Day of Reckoning

Day of Reckoning

How the Far Right Declared War on Democracy

Mike Wendling

PLUTO PRESS

First published 2024 by Pluto Press
New Wing, Somerset House, Strand, London WC2R 1LA
and Pluto Press, Inc.
1930 Village Center Circle, 3-834, Las Vegas, NV 89134

www.plutobooks.com

British Library Cataloguing in Publication Data
A catalogue record for this book is available from the British Library

ISBN   978 0 7453 4971 8   Paperback
ISBN   978 0 7453 4973 2   PDF
ISBN   978 0 7453 4972 5   EPUB

This book is printed on paper suitable for recycling and made from fully
managed and sustained forest sources. Logging, pulping and manufacturing
processes are expected to conform to the environmental standards of the
country of origin.

Typeset by Stanford DTP Services, Northampton, England

Simultaneously printed in the United Kingdom and United States of America

Contents

1. An encounter at the end of the world   1
2. *2000 Mules* and the long "Big Lie"   19
3. The murder excuse ballads   28
4. QAnon lives on and on   48
5. Proud Boys and "groomers"   59
6. Anti-vaccine derangement syndrome   71
7. No political solution   83
8. Christian nationalists and radical moms   96
9. The perpetual influencer machine   106
10. Revenge of the normies   121
Conclusion: Day of reckoning   135

Acknowledgments   151
Notes   153
Further reading   180
Index   182

1

An encounter at the
end of the world

Trego is one of those places that feels like the end of the world.

To get to this small community in north-west Montana, you drive an hour north up US Highway 93 from Kalispell, the closest town of any note, turn left before the Canadian border, and head through a thick forest. Where the side road hits train tracks there's a clearing with spectacular views of green-covered mountains.

The last US Census reported that Trego is home to 855 people, most of whom live up in these mountains, in houses, homesteads and cabins carved out of the Kootenai National Forest.

If you're unlucky, like I was when our small crew visited one afternoon in October 2022, the Trego general store, pub and post office will all be closed. We snapped a few pictures: the train tracks, the buildings, an American flag flapping away on a pole attached to a rusting tractor.

It was quiet and, except for an occasional autumn gust rolling down the Rockies, it was peaceful and still. It's hard to believe that anything in Trego could be more dramatic than the scenery looked. But we had been drawn to this stretch of wilderness by a dark, compelling story.

Trego was once the headquarters of the militia which spearheaded the most organized attempt to halt the transfer of presidential power on January 6, 2021. High in the hills was the former home of Stewart Rhodes, founder and president of the Oath Keepers, a house that had once been surrounded by trenches and booby traps.

None of Trego's 855 residents were around. Even if we did happen to encounter one, we'd been warned that not everyone in the area would be particularly chatty.

Fortunately, there was one former resident who was ready to talk to us.

Dakota Adams was the estranged son of Stewart Rhodes. Later that day, a few miles away,[1] he told me about his escape from his father.

His childhood and adolescence had tracked the growth of the Oath Keepers — from an idea to an organization to an engine of far-right revolution. The teenage Dakota, like so many young men, had strained to win the approval of his father. He participated in weapons drills and militia meetings. But then he became disillusioned. His father was angry and abusive, he said. He wanted out, and he engineered the family's escape from their Trego home.

"I spent two years scheming behind Stewart's back," he told me, "saving money to secure a lawyer and independent transportation, to make a clean getaway."

He carried out the plan on a frigid February day in 2018. Dakota and his mother made an excuse — they were going to get rid of some old junk at a nearby dump. In reality, they'd piled as many of their personal belongings as they could in the car, along with Dakota's siblings and their dog John-Boy.

Just before they took off, however, Stewart Rhodes emerged from the house. There was a brief moment of stomach-churning tension as he motioned to his son and wife. Was their plan about to be thwarted?

"Hey," Rhodes said. "Pick up some steak on your way back."

Dakota nodded, then stepped on the gas. As he sped towards Highway 93, Dakota didn't look in the rearview mirror.

When I met Dakota four and a half years later, I was struck by his determination, his eloquence – growing up, he had never attended a formal school – and his incisive comments about America's far-right currents, a political flow that had engulfed and upended his family.

Wearing a T-shirt with a picture of an anime character, with a mass of curly blonde hair spilling over his shoulders, Dakota showed us his AR-15 rifle, which he had used to kill deer to feed his family – at times in the recent past, he told me, they had been "very, very poor." We knew it would make good footage. Guns were a constant source of fascination for audiences, particularly ones outside the United States. But Dakota also told me of his deep ambivalence about firearms.

"I have absolutely no idea whether I like shooting or like being a gun nerd," he told me. Unlike many Americans, his weapons didn't make him feel very safe. It would be hard to stop any deranged militia member seeking some sort of twisted revenge, and he had very little to steal, just a few possessions in a small one-room rented apartment over a garage, with a microwave and a hotplate to cook with. The bathroom had no door.

He was in a perilous place, at a perilous time, living close to the community which had accommodated his father and his father's militia. Day-to-day, he was just trying to hold on – working to support the rest of his family, taking classes at a community college, blogging about his experiences in the militia world, working on his art, and every so often when his schedule allowed it, giving interviews to visiting reporters.

The apocalyptic thinking of his upbringing was hard to overcome, and he was carefully watching current events. As we spoke, his father was standing trial in Washington on charges including seditious conspiracy – using force "to prevent, hinder, or delay the execution of any law of the United States." In plain language, trying to keep Donald Trump in the White House.

Rhodes was among more than a thousand rioters arrested for the Capitol riot. It was one of the biggest criminal investigations in US history. And yet, even years later, even in the wilderness of northwest Montana, the threat of violence still hung heavy in the air.

"In this town about once a month, I will hear people talking about the need to go door to door and execute Democrats to fix the country," he said. "They talk about their desire for Trump's inner circle to overthrow the government and institute a right-wing, authoritarian, one-party state that will simply eliminate all opposition."

He paused for a moment and gazed at his firearms, still laid out on his bed among his martial arts awards and a few other scattered possessions.

"I have been seriously struggling with the question of whether to finally get rid of all this. It's dirty and dusty from years of storage," he said, pointing to a set of body armor.

"But I also have absolutely no confidence in the future course of this country," he told me. "And I generally have little confidence in the ability of the United States to cope with a rising fascist movement that is being excused and downplayed at every turn to preserve an illusion – the illusion of life as normal."

Not too long ago, I would have dismissed Dakota's concerns as exaggeration, paranoia, or as a very specific reaction to his unique situation. And even though I've been studying the American far right for years, particularly in its new, highly online forms, I would have seen his father – who wore an eyepatch after a gun accident – as a cartoonish character, a villain from the fringes, but far from the centers of power, with little influence beyond his own band of heavily armed men.

But soon after I moved back to the United States in the late summer of 2022, I had started to realize that the country I had left more than two decades earlier was facing a novel, strange and hyperactive internal threat – potentially much more serious than any in recent history.

My time abroad was punctuated by frequent reporting trips back to the country of my birth and encounters with all sorts of extremists and novel political actors: alt-righters, neo-Nazis, anti-government agitators, culture warriors, Proud Boys, anti-fascists, Islamist extremists.

And in years of covering the online far right, I had witnessed once-vanquished ideas travel from those fringes to unexpected places. On a beach in India I met a teenager who posted memes about the Unabomber and Pepe the Frog. One expert said there were a million kids like him, all over India – Hindu nationalists inspired by the online antics of their American cousins. In the back of a van traveling through the streets of Kinshasa, the son of an aid worker outlined, *sotto voce*, his thoughts on the proper roles of the immutable white and black races. And throughout the Covid-19 pandemic, marchers spouting anti-vaccine paranoia and American culture war hype regularly traipsed through the streets of London, accusing journalists and doctors of trampling on their freedom and insisting that there were millions in their ranks. Instead, their movement fizzled away like a wafting cloud as Britain's byzantine Covid laws lifted, leaving only the most hard-core dregs behind.

On the surface, in my new home in my old country, there was little evidence of a country gripped by extremist fever. In our neighborhood the bumper stickers and the yard signs agreed on LGBTQ+ rights and anti-racism, support for besieged Ukrainians and the Democratic Party. The main ideological split seemed to be between those who had kept their Hillary Clinton stickers from 2016 and those who preferred the socialism of Bernie Sanders.

Here, the far-right fringes seemed far away. Very occasionally I heard an acquaintance or stranger repeat some Alex Jones talking point, drop a debunked anti-vaccine tidbit into conversation, or – usually ironically – speculate that questioning some supposed orthodoxy might get them cancelled.

Ads were running on local TV stations plugging candidates in the upcoming midterm elections. Many featured the candidates' views on abortion or mentioned the cost of fruits and vegetables. In the autumn of 2022, rampant inflation dominated the news. In Detroit Metro airport, while changing planes, my children found a sticker featuring a picture of a pointing Joe Biden printed with the phrase "I DID THAT." The decals, printed by Biden's critics – there were various and many – were meant to be stuck on gas pumps positioned with the flat president gesturing at the price per gallon. Nothing in American politics is more normie than arguments over gas prices.

But this surface world was something of an illusion. The remnants of what remained of the alt-right weren't vanquished, and weren't even hibernating. In online spaces, in further-flung towns, even in Congress, they were gathering strength, staking their immediate hopes on one man and preparing for the battle ahead. Along the way they had lost much of the freewheeling spirit that made them so appealing to younger extremely online conservatives. A dark mood had taken over after Donald Trump was voted out of office. At the same time they had made steady progress towards power, in small towns and in the halls of Congress. Conspiratorial thinking had taken over the far-right fringes, and the far right was becoming increasingly mainstream.

The movement that dominates the right-wing fringes today has its roots in the political movement known as the alt-right.

This broad collection of activists began to really coalesce a decade or more ago, around what they saw as a set of fundamental issues facing the United States. Beyond their steadfast support for Donald Trump, they were motivated by a sense that they were losing control to censorious political correctness and a corrupt political system.

Alt-right activists differed in their tactics, and they ranged widely in the extent of their extremism and predilection for fighting words and actual violence. They were angry at feminists and foreigners. They were sworn enemies of radical Islam. Even as many professed to be tolerant of a wide variety people as long as they agreed with them politically, they believed that left-wing ideas about social justice and equality had compromised their country – perhaps fatally. They believed in a mostly white or white-dominated America – some went further and wanted an all-white America – and they thought they were losing their grip on power, and fast. In as much as they had an economic policy, they believed in a nationalistic form of capitalism that embraced state support for in-groups (the elderly, citizens, American corporations, white people) and eschewed China and foreign influence.

There were, to be sure, differences in emphasis, but these policy goals were outlined in blog posts and policy papers, covered on fringe news sites and social media accounts, pumped up by childish memes and goofball 4chan trolls, and imbibed by millions, including at the very extreme end, mass murderers who left angry manifestos and tried to broadcast their slaughters live on the internet.

When Donald Trump made his foray into electoral politics, these disparate groups set aside most of their differences for a moment and rallied around the man they thought of as their standard bearer. He was willing to say anything. He was brash, offensive, and triggered people online. In the eyes of most alt-righters, Trump wasn't the perfect candidate, but he was pretty damn close.

His victory in the 2016 presidential election posed a dilemma, however. The alt-right was an oppositional, radical movement that thrived on the outside, and now it had a foothold in power. Even before Trump took office, the leaderless movement started to fracture around particularly tricky questions. Should they continue to embrace extremists like Richard Spencer, the white nationalist in designer clothes who shouted to his supporters "Hail Trump" and was answered back with Nazi salutes? Why did their hero back away from throwing Hillary Clinton in prison? Why did he continue to order American troops to conduct overseas operations? And while Pizzagate – a bizarre conspiracy theory that claimed that Democrats were running a child abuse ring out of a Washington restaurant[2] – was useful for needling opponents and ramping up the base, was it really a good idea to push all this clearly crazy shit online? Disappointment was guaranteed.

While the alt-right fractured and reformed, then splintered again, three dramatic events during Trump's time in office fundamentally changed the trajectory of the American far-right.

The first was the bloody weekend of August 11 and 12, 2017 in Charlottesville, Virginia. A wide range of extremist and fringe groups attended the Unite the Right rally, and for a brief moment they looked like they might draw in even more supporters with stark images of white men carrying torches through the dark to defend a Confederate statute.

But violent clashes and the killing of a counter-protester laid bare the naked hate of the assembly, and Trump's false-equivalence response – his famous line about "very fine people on both sides" – prompted a backlash. Faced with the opportunity to put space between MAGA ("Make America Great

Again") and an even more hard-core nationalist movement, Trump decided to draw the line, well, nowhere at all.

For many Americans, this was the moment when the alt-right brand officially became toxic. Faster than it had blown up into public consciousness, it began to dissolve.

But the energy that fueled it was still present, and needed somewhere to go. Some of the anger was channeled into extremism – a shifting array of neo-Nazi and white supremacist groups, and a larger miasma of hate which subsequently produced so-called "lone wolf" mass murderers and violent attacks.

Then came the second big event – the pandemic.

Covid not only exposed America's health inequalities, it demonstrated how anything, even something as simple as wearing a cloth mask, could be politicized. Trump's administration alternately boosted the profile of US public health officials and undermined their messages. But the real political impact of the virus came far away from Washington, where the stress of the pandemic, the associated Covid rules, and an eager anti-vaccine and natural health movement stoked suspicion and distrust. And it wasn't just Trump supporters who bought into shadowy conspiratorial narratives during Covid's spread.

The third event that ushered in the next phase of America's fringe far-right was of course the riot at the US Capitol on January 6, 2021.

Like the other two watershed events, there appeared to be briefly a window of unity, a widespread revulsion at the scenes of mayhem, and even the glimpse of a possibility that had excited much of liberal America for years – the prospect of a final vanquishing of MAGA.

But before too long, Jan. 6 devolved into another political Rorschach test, a further point of division. Today a hardened minority of Americans think the rioters were generally

9

peaceful heroes defending traditional values, along with a few bear-mace spraying, cop bashing, flagpole-wielding rogues.

It's an eye-opening feat of cognitive dissonance, but the truth is the mob was fueled by conspiratorial narratives about voting and the true winner of the 2020 election. They came to Washington hoping to overturn the result, and in the intervening years those who have clung to that narrative have constructed conspiracy theories about federal agents, antifa instigators and deep state plots that continue to drive their efforts to downplay, excuse or simply wave away the events of that day.

The idea that violent protests are planned and carried out not by far-right political activists but by agents of the state is not new. Similar rumors were rife in fringe conspiracy circles after Charlottesville, for instance.[3] But now they were no longer confined to the margins. They were broadcast on Fox News and its upstart competitors, repeated by members of Congress and spread to conservative bubbles – and more than a few left-wing ones – through podcasts and social media.

Charlottesville blew the alt-right to the winds like so many dandelion seeds. The pandemic baked conspiracy and paranoia into the far right and gave it supporters in unlikely political spaces. The Capitol riot, and the evolving reaction to it, galvanized this new movement and ensured that conspiracy theories had truly arrived in the mainstream of American political life.

Once ensconced in the Midwest, I made it my mission to try to find out as much as I could about this new fringe politics – to travel around the country, talk to people, scroll through hundreds and hundreds of posts and videos. Who made up the far right, and what did they believe?

Like the alt-right that preceded it, this movement is incredibly nebulous. It has champions in Congress, particularly in a bloc of around 40–50 Republicans known as the House Freedom Caucus, and various elected officials at all levels of government. But it's networked, mostly leaderless beyond Trump, and is full of competing interests, attention-seekers, grifters, shady anonymous characters and random hangers-on.

Also like the old alt-right, it's far from cohesive, and riddled with infighting and beefs, both personal and ideological. In some places, its subgroups overlap heavily. It lacks an umbrella term or even a proper name.[4] That not only makes it hard to delineate and quantify, but easy for its proponents to deflect criticism or go on the attack when observers make slight mistakes in categorizing, labeling or grouping people together.

Trump's most enthusiastic supporters are a central group, particularly those who still buy fully into what's become known as the "Big Lie" – the idea that widespread voter fraud swung the 2020 election. As I'll show, the Big Liars are not simply relying on blind faith. They have their own piles of "evidence," their own expert networks and political organizations, and their own ecosystem devoted to "voter integrity" that has proved impervious to years of outside scrutiny. Not only do they believe that one election was rigged, they increasingly believe that the whole system is utterly broken.

A broader mass of conspiratorial thinkers – or, in their own minds, free thinkers or free speech champions – are another key element. They have taken the idea, useful to critical thinkers, that sometimes governments, media reports and authority figures are wrong, and they have set an extreme version of it in stone: the authorities are *always* wrong. The media *lies*. All experts are *bad*.

They include in their number some very rich and powerful people, and nowhere is their warped thinking more on display than in their approach to mass murder and terror attacks. They often work to undermine a true accounting of the far-right violence, and wittingly or not, deflect attention away from an extremist culture – the fringes of the alt-right and online white supremacists – that revels in violence and is working to destabilize democracy.

QAnon is another large subset. Remarkably, this conspiratorial movement has survived despite all indications that it would stall out. It has been the subject of countless exposés. "Q" himself hasn't posted for years. Yet the energy QAnon unleashed clearly spoke to many in a way that cannot entirely be explained away. For years the Trump camp has tried to keep QAnon at arm's length[5] – realizing that its political fervor was useful, but its core ideas were an embarrassment.

That period, however, is in the past. According to one estimate,[6] Trump has posted QAnon messages hundreds of times on his Truth Social account. These ranged from promoting QAnon podcasts and accounts to reposting QAnon slogans and memes to boosting popular QAnon influencer accounts – even screenshots of messages that had originally been posted by the eponymous Q himself. Trump now says the quiet part out loud.

Covid denialists are another source of furious fringe energy. Their ideas were sprawling, contradictory, led by social media rather than science. Some thought Covid was the same as the flu. Others suggested the virus didn't exist, or that viruses do not exist, at all, period. The symptoms of Covid were really being caused by 5G cell phone installations, others said, or could be cured with vitamins, or cheap drugs that the pharmaceutical companies didn't want you to have, or expensive drugs that powerful elites didn't want you to have, or bleach, or solar energy. Masks were useless, or more useful for the state than for the wearer, because they had secret microchips in them (as did vaccines) that could be used to track you, or were handy in evading facial recognition systems, and thus led to more criminal activity.

Even more extreme ideas included rumors that martial law would be imposed and lead to concentration camps where people would be turned into slaves, or be summarily executed, or that only the vaccinated population would be allowed to live freely, or that the vaccinated would drop dead because of Covid vaccines, which were magnetic, or poisonous, or completely ineffective.

This only skims the surface of the ocean of various Covid conspiracies that have circulated since March 2020. However, as bizarre and contradictory as many of these ideas are, they have a few basic concepts in common. An alliance of elites including government, business, medicine and media is attempting to seize control of fundamental aspects of your life. Anything "mainstream" is a lie; truth can only be found in contrarians online. Only you, the individual autonomous awoken free thinker can find the truth. All others who have not yet seen the light are "sheeple" under the sway of "wokism."

If you're not familiar with the conspiracy ecosystem that flowered during the pandemic, it can seem disorienting to see the legions of keyboard warriors who group together scorn of racial justice, climate change science, mainstream media outlets, the United States government, big business and vaccination, sometimes all in the same tweet. But they believe they are all intimately related things, advanced in lockstep by a shadowy elite.

And like the QAnon believers, you might think that the Covid deniers would chill a little as the virus has evolved from a worldwide obsession to part of the background noise of everyday life. But again, you'd be wrong.

The Covid deniers have increasingly narrowed their focus to vaccines, and anti-vaccination activists deserve an extra special mention in our taxonomy. On the face of, they would not appear to be natural MAGA types. Donald Trump had once embraced discredited theories about links between vaccines and autism, but even he could figure out what would bring the pandemic to an end. And so he became a vocal proponent of Operation Warp Speed, one of the biggest vaccination research efforts in history.

But in an indication of the power of anti-vax ideas, even Trump could not sway the bulk of his supporters. The growing movement, along with a much larger number drawn in by their rhetoric, now means that vaccines are political in a way that perhaps they haven't been since the time of Edward Jenner. Trump has occasionally mentioned his vaccination status in front of rallies, only to be booed,[7] and his rivals for the Republican nomination have expressed varying levels of anti-vaccination sentiment.

These far-right groups are fueled, melded and amplified by growing networks of right-wing and far-right alternative media. The main characters in this space are a mix of people with big audiences, fringe characters with rabid followings, the racist rump of the old alt-right, and pundits, podcasters and tech bosses.

And there are established right-wing groups, three of which stand out for their involvement in the Capitol riot: the Proud Boys, the Oath Keepers and the Three Percenters movement. Each has a different emphasis, and they met vastly different fates after the riot. Most notably, the Proud Boys have shifted their focus and have become the vanguard for a radical anti-transgender movement, reflecting a broader trend across the right.

Counter-extremism experts often use the metaphor of a pipeline to explain how some people who have sympathy with statements like "feminism has gone too far" or "white people face discrimination" end up in extremist movements or neo-Nazi cults, through personal relationships, organizations or the effects of social media. At the far end of that pipe are the most explicitly racist and violent groups. They include

Patriot Front – a shadowy organization responsible for a staggering proportion of white supremacist propaganda across the United States today.[8]

Lurking even further back in the shadows are small cells and individuals plotting accelerationist violence – mass murders and attacks against the nation's power grid. These are underground extremists who hold the most radical views, and have some of the greatest potential for spawning mass violence. Of all the groups I've listed, you'd think these radicals would be the easiest to categorize and, across the broader right, a slam dunk to condemn. But conspiratorial ideas have been so baked into the national political conversation – and some activists are determined to cling to the notion that there are "no enemies to the right" – that they have concocted elaborate theories to explain away even the most frightening groups and heinous crimes.

These accelerationists pose a particular threat as political chaos ramps up. They are motivated by the idea that their goals can be accomplished by speeding up social change through violence and extreme action until things spin entirely out of control, at which point they plan to seize the moment and reshape the world according to their beliefs. Only by pushing society past the breaking point, they say, will a new order arise from the ashes of the old. There are right-wing and left-wing flavors of this idea,[9] and it's not entirely new, particularly among white nationalists. But accelerationist currents are strengthening on the far right, and the 2024 election provides another pivotal moment where extremists may try to blow open society's cracks with violence.

The problems presented by the American far right would be eminently manageable if they were confined to the margins. But just at the point where they have become darker and more conspiratorial, these fringes have also managed to establish footholds in many levels of government.

There are QAnon boosters in Congress, Proud Boys getting involved in school board politics, and conspiracy theorists getting elected to offices up and down the country. In many cases they're doing so not by hiding their fringe tendencies, but by emphasizing them – collecting the votes of millions who think a vast conspiracy is arrayed against them.

These are Trump's people, and they empathize with their hero because they believe he's being wronged, just as they've been wronged – by experts, by vaccines, by progressives, by the deep state or by the Democrat down the road. The ideas that maintain Trump and his comrades, once seen as fringe, are now part of the mainstream of the Republican Party, and once again all of the disparate groups that make up America's far-right fringes are gearing up to put aside their differences and back their man.

Conspiracy has overtaken the American far right, and the American far right has crept into the mainstream.

In one of our intense, lengthy conversations in Montana, Dakota Adams told me how his father, the Oath Keepers leader, was able to ride a decade of anger and doubt to become one of the leaders of a force that almost toppled a government.

"The crest in the wave came at exactly the right moment," he told me, "which is how the Oath Keepers catapulted from a draft blog post from a guy who's on the verge of being evicted for nonpayment of rent, whose children don't have any food, to being a national figure."

Not only had Dakota grown up in the militia movement, but he'd also spent plenty of time online – as a homeschooled kid in rural Montana was likely to do – including on 4chan, fringe message boards and some of the other worst places on the internet, along with more mundane spaces.

"I was spending most of my time hiding from the reality that I thought I lived in, one of imminent total societal collapse," he said.

He told me a story about a time before his escape, when he was deeply involved in an online role-playing game, acting as a dungeon master, until all of a sudden, he was interrupted by his father and some neighbors in Trego. They'd found a boot print they didn't recognize nearby and suspected an intrusion by FBI agents or enemies with a beef. It was all systems go.

"I had to throw on that body armor in the middle of the night, get my rifle ready," Dakota recalled. "I had to make sure I had armor piercing rounds loaded, make sure I had a scope with a night vision setting."

They combed the land around the house in Trego, checked the trenches and the booby traps. The boot mark turned out to be from one of the militiamen themselves. Jacked up on paranoia, he'd failed to recognize his own footprint.

Paranoia warps the mind, heightens our sense of danger and drama, and makes us see threats where there are none. Dakota knew the life of a paranoiac. And now he knows the people he is wary of are not the stuff of legend, mistaken boot prints or elaborate conspiracy theories, even as he admitted he was confused about exactly how much of a threat they pose to the fabric of American democracy.

"I have no idea from inside my own head what is a pre-programmed response from years of paranoia and conspiracy theory that I absorbed as a child, and what is reality," he told me. "I don't know if the headlines are simply triggering my apocalypse reflex, or if we are actually in serious danger."

"And while I'm uncertain, I'm not going to be getting rid of this," he said, gesturing again at his guns and body armor.

"Considering the state of the nation," he said, "I feel like I should be training."

In May 2023, Stewart Rhodes was sentenced to 18 years in prison for his role in the Capitol riot. If his legal appeals fail, Dakota told me, Rhodes is likely pinning his hopes for early release on Donald Trump regaining the White House and issuing pardons to the rioters – something the former president has repeatedly said he would do, albeit in vague terms.[10]

For Stewart Rhodes,[11] a Trump victory might be the difference between freedom and imprisonment, but millions view what's at stake in the next presidential election in terms even more stark. They believe their country is being stolen from them by extremist forces: a blob they and Trump call communist, fascist, antifa, woke, globalist or dozens of other labels, sometimes all at once. Trump himself encapsulated this thinking in a speech in New Hampshire in December 2023, where he promised to "root out the communists, Marxists, fascists and the radical left thugs that live like vermin within the confines of our country that lie and steal and cheat on elections."

Even though they are large in number, these millions are mostly invisible to large parts of liberal America. They hold most of their power far from the big cities and talk amongst themselves in their podcast circuits and in their own safe spaces online. In other places they are so completely mainstream that they blend into the background; in many states and counties they have become the Republican Party establishment.

In the coming pages, I'll explore who these people are and how they have made some of their once-fringe ideas central to the exercise of American politics today. And to begin with, I'll outline how, above all, they are propelled by that so-called Big Lie, the one that inspired the Capitol riot – the idea that Donald Trump was the true winner of the 2020 presidential election.

2

2000 Mules and the long "Big Lie"

In 2022, the top grossing documentary[1] in American movie theatres was *Moonage Daydream*, a film about David Bowie. In second place was a movie called *2000 Mules*.

It was written by and starred Dinesh D'Souza, a longtime conservative pundit who was pardoned by Donald Trump after he pleaded guilty to violating federal election law.

2000 Mules opens with a clip of Joe Biden, from a podcast broadcast just before the 2020 election. He says: "We have put together I think the most extensive and inclusive voter fraud organization in the history of American politics."

Biden was talking about the team of lawyers he'd assembled to fight against doubts that Donald Trump had already been spreading for months – alleging that the voting system was unfair and rigged against him. It was a piece of garbled syntax from a man who's known for it, and not, as many suggested, a public revelation of a nefarious plot to steal an election.[2] However, in the context of the movie, it fit perfectly into the preconceived notion of Trump's biggest supporters and many on the right – that the election was stolen, and the democratic process could not be trusted.

This fiction was hatched by Trump and has proved to be stubbornly persistent, with about a third of Americans believing in it.[3] It's not confined to the margins; one of its chief proponents, Congressman Mike Johnson, was elected in

October 2023 to be Speaker of the House. The idea that Trump really and truly won the election has proved to be impervious to debunks and fact checks. Distrust in the electoral system is the cornerstone of America's conspiratorial far right, the foundation that their political worldview is built upon.

Even though many news organizations have thoroughly debunked the film's shaky assertions,[4] the movie is instructive – in the specific case of how Trump's personal nosedive into the Big Lie story has become central to America's far right, but also as a demonstration of how conspiracy theories work as powerful vectors of propaganda. Although it didn't exactly win any major awards, watching *2000 Mules* is at times actually quite an engrossing experience, and if you put yourself in the shoes of a Trump supporter, you can see how it could be both emotionally stirring and deeply convincing.

After the Biden clip at the very start, D'Souza, the very picture of a political wonk, intones about democracy and assembles a panel of conservative talking heads who express various degrees of skepticism and belief in the Big Lie. The real meat comes when viewers are introduced to the leaders of an organization called True The Vote – experts, the audience is told, in sniffing out election fraud.

True The Vote obtained masses of cell phone records – billions of blips of data depicted by kinetic graphics splashing across the frame – which allowed them to map the movements of millions of people. They found that in 2020, many people in American cities passed by ballot drop boxes on a number of occasions, and also passed by the offices of left-leaning not-for-profit voter organizations.

Both ballot drop boxes and offices are often located in high-traffic urban areas. But from this mundane fact, the makers of *2000 Mules* – already predisposed, mind you, to think something fishy's going on – leap to a startling assumption: these anonymous people are picking up large numbers of fraudulent ballots that workers at the not-for-profits have "harvested," and dropping them off in the boxes.

The truth is crystal clear – that is, if you already believe that the election was rigged.

To bolster their case, the filmmakers also obtained some video clips of people putting multiple ballots into drop boxes. Having assumed with fuzzy back-of-the-envelope math that ballot "mules" exist – as the title implies, at least 2,000 of them – D'Souza[5] infers that he has found the actual cheaters.

With one exception – which I'll return to in a moment – there's precious little in *2000 Mules* that rises above low-level circumstantial evidence, in the way that police detectives or investigative journalists understand that term. None of the fraudulent ballots are produced. The mechanism by which fictional voters are created out of thin air and issued with ballots isn't described in any detail. There are no in-depth interviews with insiders or whistleblowers or people with deep knowledge of the alleged scheme filling in the details of how the "fraud" was allegedly carried out, no intercepted emails or phone conversations with Democratic Party operatives contacting not-for-profit "vote mule" operations. The investigation consists of millions of phone records in high-density urban areas, and videos of some people dropping off multiple ballots, presumably those of friends and family members.

At one point Catherine Engelbrecht, True The Vote's co-founder, tries to explain away the lack of eyewitnesses to the fakery by claiming people are afraid to speak out because they are "scared they're going to be cancelled." In another section, demonstrating a strange ignorance of the deep splits in the American left, the movie implies that many of the "mules," who are supposedly working for mainstream organizations in service to the Democratic Party, are also violent activists, or antifa or Black Lives Matter operatives.

That one exception to the film's lack of solid evidence is an interview with an anonymous receptionist at an unnamed organization based in Yuma County, Arizona. She is, we are led to believe, one of the mules. She speaks of delivering hundreds of ballots to a library drop box. She expresses concern that she unwittingly and illegally helped to alter the course of American history.

Here, finally, the filmmakers are on to something. It turns out there are credible allegations of fraud and machine-style politics in San Luis, a Yuma County city of about 25,000 people. Several people were subsequently charged with illegal ballot harvesting, among them a former mayor who was convicted and sentenced to a month in jail.[6]

But a closer look reveals that at the most, this was an isolated story of small-town corruption. It certainly did not have an impact on the 2020 presidential election. A majority of voters in Yuma County voted for Trump in 2020. In fact, he chalked up an even bigger victory[7] there than the win he managed to eke out in 2016.

Somehow the effect of the purported plot – in the very place where the makers of *2000 Mules* had found their most convincing evidence, real proof of fraud – was the exact opposite of what might be expected.

This anomaly joined the list of awkward truths that Big Lie proponents carefully elide. One of the biggest ones is the result of down-ballot races in 2020. Somehow the Republican Party managed to make significant gains in Congress at the same time as a massive alleged Democratic Party voter fraud operation was rigging the presidency. None of the conspiracists have quite managed to explain how that happened.

Critically examined, the evidence in the film does not back up its intended conclusion. But *2000 Mules* was released against a background of already-entrenched suspicion in the voting process. There was no need to fill in some of the more obvious gaps in the narrative. The beliefs about rampant corruption and subversion of the will of the people which were once so common in left-wing movements had found their answer on the right. It meant that most of the intended audience skipped over the holes, ignored the fact-checkers and got engrossed in the good stuff – flashy graphics and convincing testimony about pervasive fraud.

Like most conspiracy theories, vote fraud theories contain kernels of truth and incorporate facts – in this case, the cell phone and mapping data, which there's no reason to doubt – to bolster their case and provide a pre-emptive cudgel with which to poke back at critics, something like: "You call us conspiracy theorists, but how do you explain this?"

And thinly evidenced conspiracy theories can really catch on if there are millions of people primed to believe in them. For a stubborn and sizeable portion of Trump supporters, the Big Lie is preferable to the truth: For a significant subset of their fellow Americans – enough to swing an election – Donald Trump is unpopular and divisive.

The film's casual mention of other conspiracy theories fits into the "red-pilled" mindset. This is an idea based on a scene from another film, *The Matrix*, that reality is not what it seems. Through one decision – choosing to take the "red pill" of uncomfortable truth rather than the "blue pill" of soothing lies – you can free your mind and see reality for what it truly is.

This is fiction, of course, but the idea that you can choose to see reality or not has caught on in meme-like fashion. It explains how people who are led down rabbit holes can come to believe they are really seeking the truth. Political beliefs can inform conspiracy thinking, and people who buy into one conspiracy theory, experts say, often buy into others.[8]

Joseph Uscinski, one of the leading experts in the academic field of conspiracy research, pointed out to me that conspiracy thinking "exists both on the left and the right and about in equal amounts."

"For example, during Obama's presidency it seemed like the right was a bunch of conspiracy cranks. But when you look during Republican presidencies, Democrats are engaging in conspiracy theories quite a bit too," he said.[9]

Americans on the left of politics bought into conspiratorial ideas after Hillary Clinton's defeat. Fake news stories written by Macedonian teenagers were blamed for her loss, as were Russian meddling, the FBI, the media, Democratic Party strategy and other things.[10] Lawsuits were filed to force recounts in several states. But those efforts ebbed away. No government buildings were stormed. The candidate herself left the national political stage.

However, the mere fact that there was some fairly loud dispute after the 2016 election is regularly used as an argument by right-wing fringe characters in order to justify their own ongoing obsession with vote fraud.[11] In the next chapter I'll explore how this strategy of trying to flip the script against political opponents is used in even darker circumstances – in the wake of mass murders committed by ideological extremists.

And another key difference emerged after Donald Trump captured the White House, Uscinski noted: "Now you have Trump supporters getting into conspiracy theories too, because Trump is actively pushing them – because that's his mantra."

Conspiracy theories can act as a balm to the powerless, assuaging their fears that the world is random, or that their misfortune or the misfortune of those around them are the fault of grand forces, that fighting against those they perceive as elites is a quest for the ages. But when they're pushed by the powerful, they become dangerous. They can turn mobs against scapegoats and consolidate the power of dictators. We're now in another period of American history – there have been several – where conspiracy thinking is at the forefront of our politics, and its proponents are struggling to gain the upper hand. Those who acknowledge reality have so far offered little effective pushback to the conspiracists. Fact-checking has not appeared to make much of a dent in their beliefs. There are very few advocates for some relatively minor changes to voter ID laws or moves towards paper ballots that could potentially peel off the more rational thinkers and politically isolate the conspiracists. It's fair to say that at the time of writing, there's not yet any effective political strategy for combating the Big Lie.

The consequences could be very grave. D'Souza ends *2000 Mules* by intoning very simply: "They rigged and stole the 2020 election."

The movie was fairly popular – its backers claimed that one million people had seen it in the two weeks after release[12] – however, *2000 Mules* was but one drop in a huge stream of content designed to back up the long Big Lie. For many, belief in voter fraud theories has become an article of quiet faith, and there will always be a committed minority within that group who are ready to act.

On January 6, 2021, we got an idea of what that committed minority might do. The trials of the major players during the Capitol riot got deeply in the weeds with arguments about the meaning of messages, whether participants thought they were following Donald Trump's orders, and important legal questions about what the rioters set out to do and what they themselves hoped to achieve by invading Congress.

But at a more basic level, one belief united them all: they thought the election was rigged. They thought Trump won. They wanted him to stay in the White House.

Although he consistently defended the rioters, D'Souza met a vastly different fate than those who actually carried out the attack. He continued to rake in money with his podcasts, films and other output. In June 2023, he invited Stewart Rhodes onto his show, introducing him by saying: "He's being held as a political prisoner in a DC jail."

"I think the judge at sentencing, the mask came off. He made it very clear I was being punished for my free speech," Rhodes said.[13] The Oath Keepers leader continued to believe his own propaganda. Gently prodded by D'Souza, Rhodes spun a tale of the justice system being hopelessly stacked against him, all of the judges – even the Trump-appointed ones – moving in lockstep, a tainted Washington jury pool. At one point he compares the situation in America today to that of Germany in the 1930s.

"We have never seen such a travesty of justice on such a mass scale," D'Souza agreed. He floated the possibility of an appeal, but neither man appeared to hold out much hope of its success. Rhodes signed off by thanking D'Souza and saying: "The Constitution was violated in the 2020 election."

The beliefs of the pro-Trump conspiracists hadn't faded over time – in fact, some hard-core believers found their faith growing even stronger as movies and podcasts and social media feeds filled up with "proof" and "evidence."

Later, I would discover how the general idea of "election fraud" had started to poison the entire political system, ending up infecting politics in small towns around the country, even ones where Republicans had overwhelming electoral advantages.

And it's not hard to follow the map to the dark place where these ideas might lead. If you believe in 2020 election fraud conspiracy theories, there's no reason to believe the system would be any fairer in 2024, with a Democrat in the White House. And if peaceful protest was fruitless and even a riot didn't "stop the steal," what would you be prepared to do next time?

These are uncomfortable questions. To much of the country, election denial seemed to be old news, even as it was shaping up to be a main theme of the 2024 contest. And most of those who believed in such theories were not themselves violent, even if they condoned the mob that stormed the Capitol and beat police officers. But alongside the increasingly conspiratorial bent of the fringe right, a violent streak was beginning to harden, driven by extremists and radicalized online spaces. The new dynamics of American domestic terrorism had their roots in the Obama years and began to play out, violently, under Trump. This trend posed difficulties for more mainstream figures who wanted to cast their movement as peaceful. But there was already a strategy shaping up to overcome that obstacle – an upside-down logic that was working to try to ensure that even the most horrific crimes would not politically dent the MAGA movement.

3

The murder excuse ballads

In late September 2017 the weather in northern California was sunny and mild – in fact, positively blissful. Students had been back on the UC-Berkeley campus for a few weeks, but the autumn sun seemed to make them drift languidly to and from classes, even as a dramatic series of rolling protests and fights buzzed around them.

I went to Berkeley to cover clashes over a provocative speaking series held by a conservative group – alt-right and right-wing speakers invited to a famously left-wing university. Since the election of Donald Trump, the Berkeley campus had been revived as a focal point in American arguments over freedom of speech. A mix of student activists, locals and outside agitators held rallies and protests that frequently collapsed into fights and melees. Alt-right groups poured into town from up and down the West Coast and were met by black-clad antifa activists. The anarchists smashed windows, and the two factions bashed each other with fists and sticks.

The latest trigger point was dubbed "free speech week" and was scheduled just six weeks after the violence in Charlottesville, Virginia. While none of the groups were carrying firearms, at least openly – California's gun laws are strict – they came to campus toting a variety of makeshift weapons, batons, flagpoles, shields and cans of pepper spray. All sorts of weapons would be used that week.

Berkeley's mayor told me that authorities were getting a grip on the situation and were determined to prevent violence.

That was easier said than done. The marches and speeches and attempted speeches were spread out over the course of several days, and even the events planned well in advance spawned spontaneous offshoots and side battles.

We followed anti-fascists as they occupied a campus building and set off the fire alarms, and tailed after Proud Boys and other assorted far-right figures as they stormed a communist bookstore. We had planned a day of shooting protest material and the rest of the time collecting thoughtful interviews, but ended up spending most of the week chasing crowds, the smells of sweat, metal and pepper spray lingering in the air. The mood was one of chaos.

At one point during a lull in the proceedings, our crew paused to observe the scene outside a campus building, next to two people who were also toting cameras and recording equipment. It seemed like a safe space from which to observe. They were excited when I told them we were from the BBC and had flown from London.

"We're journalists too," one of them replied. "I'm a reporter for the Red Elephants."

The outlet was unfamiliar to me, but we had a polite conversation.[1] Our chat turned to the events in Charlottesville.

"It's not like the media would have you believe," she said. "Heather Heyer died of a heart attack. You should look into it."

"It's true," her companion piped up. "It's right there in the autopsy. Nobody wants to report it. Censored."

This was false; Heyer's autopsy report[2] clearly states that she died of blunt force trauma to the torso.

But that conversation in Berkeley was the first inkling that I had of a new trend on the conspiratorial right, the first time I had heard someone actually say that particular conspiracy theory, which had been circulating on right-wing blogs and social media, out loud.

And similar rumors were repeated with increasing frequency over the next few years, so often that I came to think of them collectively as a discreet strategy: "murder denial." It was, as it turned out, just one of a range of rhetorical tactics that have become almost default responses in the wake of far-right terror attacks.

Throughout the course of the 2016 presidential campaign, the alt-right had a ready-made excuse for overt references to violence and racism splashed all over their favorite online hangouts: *it's just a joke*.[3]

Nobody in the movement was really intent on violence, this argument went, and the few that were serious about bloodshed were immediately expunged from the movement, and anyway, these losers were unserious cast-outs who rarely emerged from their mothers' basements and posed little danger to larger society.

This narrative, tenuous to begin with, started to completely unravel in Charlottesville, when Heyer was run over by a white nationalist.

Then came the onslaught: a string of high-profile extremist terror attacks around the world inspired by alt-right and far-right ideas. They included mass murders – in Buffalo, Pittsburgh, El Paso, Colorado Springs, a shopping mall outside of Dallas, white nationalist slaughter in Christchurch and an incel attack in Toronto – many other shootings and plots, along with less-publicized attacks against people and infrastructure, thwarted plans, street brawls and battles with opposition political groups, all the way down to a significant recent spike in anti-Semitic propaganda and vandalism.

At the most violent end, not only have far-right mass killings increased over the last decade or so,[4] but law enforcement and extremism experts say the pattern indicates the far right has become the dominant domestic threat in the United States

– supplanting the danger from Islamist violence which provided a core rallying point for Trump's 2016 campaign.

This shift posed a problem for the more mainstream elements of the alt-right. They did not want to be seen as violent – in fact, they pitched themselves as peaceful, politically incorrect opponents of those they accused of being the real source of violence: extremist leftists and radical Islamists.

To deal with this problem, far-right activists began to employ a range of deflection techniques in order to downplay or dismiss the threat that extremists pose to Americans, particularly ones who are black, Hispanic, gay, transgender, Jewish or members of some other minority group.

Murder denial was one – the insistence that violence isn't really violence at all, and that deaths or seemingly violent incidents actually have different causes, often obscured by some sort of conspiratorial cover-up.

Related to this is motive denial, broadly casting doubt on evidence that crimes were motivated by far-right ideas, or trying to link them to far-left ideas instead.

And there's the old gambit of false equivalence – downplaying far-right violence by arguing that other forms of extremism are more pervasive or dangerous.

The influence of the conspiracy world has also thrown up some even more bizarre and unconventional tactics, like allegations of "deep state," "false flag," "psyop" plots. Put as simply as possible (it's hard), this is the idea that attacks are carried out or permitted to be carried out by government, "deep state," antifa, "globalist" or other unnamed actors as part of a conspiracy or "psychological operation" ("psyop") to influence public opinion – to smear those on the right, boost funding for security agencies or support for censorship, or provide a pretext for disarming American civilians.

It sounds mind-bending, but allegations of deep state false-flag psyops are now so remarkably common online that they've become almost an automatic reflex. And as I'll show, in a strange irony, this concept is deployed not just by fringe players and internet trolls, but by elite, influential members of society.

After news breaks of some sort of threat or violent incident, journalists (myself and my colleagues included) are often assigned to investigate the facts. Low-level incidents happen so often that few people are actually aware of the bulk of them, and most – bomb threats against libraries, a suspicious car at Baltimore airport, a car crashing into the Chinese consulate in San Francisco, to take just a few stories from autumn 2023 – have no proven link to extremist actors. They come and go in a blink, perhaps marked by a few short news stories.

But some of them do have a broader ideological motivation and attract more attention. And when that happens, and those stories are more widely reported, the far-right excuse machine kicks into operation.

Here's how it works.

Murder denial

This was the tactic employed by those who spread the rumor about Heyer. Other rumors tried to link the man who took the video of the attack to George Soros – with the implication that the murder was "staged" or "set up," used to maximize shock and outrage to advance leftist and left-wing concerns.

The activists driving the rumors are rarely explicit about the specifics of a plot or exact in outlining their theories about what "actually" went down. This modern mode of conspiracy is less about constructing realistic alternative worlds and more about casting shade on the perceived "official" narrative. Asking questions is enough – the goal is to sow doubt, attract attention on social media and make the rumors catch fire in the larger right-wing ecosystem. Critics or journalists who point out the flaws in the premises of the questions – or who point to evidence such as autopsy reports – are accused of censorship or closed-mindedness, of shilling for official sources or being in the pocket of elites.

It's curious, then, that murder denial is often used to defend existing power structures. Take, for instance, the persistent allegation that George Floyd died of a drug overdose – repeated for years on far-right blogs and in 2023 by former Fox News host Tucker Carlson, who cited one line in an unrelated deposition as absolute proof that Floyd was not murdered.[5]

It's true that Floyd had fentanyl and methamphetamine in his system at the time of his murder. But the local coroner, medical experts and a jury rejected claims that the drugs, rather than the police officer captured on video kneeling on his neck, were the main cause of his death.[6]

The Floyd case shows the limits of murder denial or victim blaming when these strategies come up against cold hard facts. It's hard to explain away a graphic video of an officer choking a man, bystander footage of an attack or a livestream showing a mass killing.

Of all the tactics on this list, murder denial is perhaps the one of most limited, with fairly specific use cases, and other modes of denial have become more common.

But it does show how ready some are to grasp onto a reason – any reason at all – to explain away extremist violence.

Motive denial

A man with a swastika tattoo and a "Right Wing Death Squad" patch on his clothing, who repeatedly posted neo-Nazi memes online, marched into a Texas shopping mall in May 2023 and killed nine people. After a four-minute rampage, the killer was gunned down by a local cop. Because he's dead, it's difficult to pin down exactly how far his ideology motivated his deadly actions, as against his reported mental health problems.

But many refused to believe he could have possibly been motivated by far-right propaganda, simply because of his Hispanic background. Of course, there are strong overlaps between white supremacy and Nazism, but anyone with even a glancing knowledge of Latin American politics knows that brown skin and brownshirts are not mutually exclusive.

The conspiratorial thinking spread well beyond the fringes. Twitter/X boss Elon Musk cast doubt on the facts in a message to his millions of followers.

The conspiracy theory was fueled by the unusual way the killer's writings came to light. After an oblique mention in a *New York Times* story, Aric Toler, a researcher for the open-source network Bellingcat, uncovered the material posted to a social network named Odnoklassniki, or ok.ru. Unless you speak Russian, it's likely you've never heard of it, but it's one of the country's most popular sites,[7] and is popular enough in Russia and other countries of the former Soviet Union to rank as one of the most popular social networks in the world. Furthermore, the killer also had an online footprint in a more familiar space: YouTube.

After Toler tweeted about his findings, I helped my BBC colleague Shayan Sardarizadeh double-check the material. It included pictures of Nazis, praise for Hitler, photos of the shopping mall that appeared to be reconnaissance for the attack, and other extremist material. The use of a Russian social network was unusual, but the world we currently live in is one where mass killers post their manifestos on anarchic message boards, livestream their attacks on gaming websites, and where extreme sites like 4chan and 8kun are key organizing nodes of far-right thought. For researchers working in this area, the use of a website obscure to Western observers made the discovery of the material more of a challenge, but there was no evidence that the material was not authentic. Days after the attack, police confirmed the killer's "neo-Nazi ideation."[8]

It was clear that the man was influenced by online propaganda and held fascist beliefs, but there was no convincing the conspiratorial thinkers – Musk included.

Motive denial goes beyond simply casting doubt on root causes, to actively blaming attacks on the bogeyman of the far right – progressives. Where mass killers have cited ecologically fascist or economically redistributive ideas, political partisans have pushed to paint them as leftists, left-wingers or liberals, taking advantage of the fact that many people are not intimately familiar with concepts like eco-fascism or the economic policies of fascist regimes.

Perhaps the most notable case of motive denial happened during one of the most shocking and brazen terror attacks of recent years. On May 14, 2022, news broke that a teenager had entered a grocery store in Buffalo, New York and killed ten people.

When the news broke of mass slaughter in my hometown, I was still in England. I excused myself from what until then had been a jovial dinner with friends and set out to find the killer's online footprint. He'd attempted to livestream the attack, but fortunately Twitch, the gaming site, shut down the stream after a couple of minutes.[9] Otherwise, as the pattern of previous attacks shows, the footage of the entire gruesome scene would have remained available online forever into the future.[10]

The killer's "manifesto," however, wasn't difficult to find, and amounted to hundreds of rambling pages of text and illustrations. It included a question-and-answer section. To the question "Are you 'left wing'?" he wrote: "Depending on the definition, sure." He wrote a similar answer to the question "Are you a socialist?" He also espoused views that would not be out of place in the environmental movement.

For some, these statements made for an open and shut case. Take Andy Biggs, Republican representative from Arizona and a member of the House Freedom Caucus. In December 2022, Biggs said in Congress: "We hear a lot about right-wing extremists. But this guy was an admitted socialist who was thankful that the conservative movement was dead."

But what did he leave out? Elsewhere in the document, the killer described himself as a "bigot, racist xenophobe, nazi, fascist," an "ethno-nationalist," an "eco-fascist national socialist" and even a "populist." Biggs did not mention these sections.

The Buffalo shooter was not shot dead by police, so unlike the Texas gunman, we can be much clearer about his ultimate motivations. At his sentencing hearing he said: "I shot and killed people because they were black. Looking back now, I can't believe I actually did it. I believed what I read online and acted out of hate."[11]

Any fair-minded person who takes more than a cursory look at the facts of the case and the Buffalo killer's own words would have to admit that his actions were motivated by racist, fascist ideas. It's about as clear as a case as it's possible to conceive of, but these extreme concepts have seeped so far into the mainstream right that powerful people – even members of Congress – denied the truth.

False equivalence

There are many examples of extremist violence motivated by left-wing ideologies, including a number of recent examples. Since 2016, there have been a number of attacks carried out by black separatists, anti-fascists, pro-abortion activists and other people with broadly left-wing views. Two separate attacks by black nationalists in 2016, in Texas and Louisiana, killed a total of eight police officers and injured several others.[12] And a left-wing activist killed a member of a far-right group in Portland[13] in August 2020.

But research strongly indicates that these incidents happen with much less frequency than neo-Nazi and white suprem-acist murders and mass killings. And in recent years another pattern has emerged – most of the highest-profile attacks inspired by left-wing ideas have generally been less serious compared with violence perpetuated by the fringe right. In some cases, related to some issues – like the pro-abortion movement – the attacks mostly consist of vandalism against buildings and pregnancy centers run by anti-abortion groups.

A number of studies have identified right-wing violence as the major domestic terrorism threat facing the United States. The research is clear, and it points in one direction. It includes reports by the Center for Strategic and International Studies,[14] the Anti-Defamation League,[15] the Brookings Institution,[16] the Council on Foreign Relations,[17] New America,[18] notes from the Department of Homeland Security,[19] the FBI,[20] the Government Accountability Office,[21] academic experts[22] and others. Experts, including those at the Program on Extremism at George Washington University, note that research into left-wing extremism has been sullied by political arguments – and they point out that there is definitely a potential for a rise in anarchist and left-wing violence in response to political polar-ization and domestic terror activity on the right.[23] But even those who argue that violence perpetrated by left-wingers is a significant problem go out of their way to avoid comparisons with the scale of right-wing attacks.[24]

Yet polling shows that Trump voters and Republicans, egged on by far-right activists who successfully highlight cases of anti-fascist and other left-wing violence on social media, see a finely balanced picture when it comes to recent attacks. Around half say that they come mostly from left-wing activists.[25] Tucker Carlson, while he was a host on Fox News and shortly after the El Paso attack, declared that, far from a public safety issue or a real social problem, white supremacy is "a conspiracy theory used to divide the country and keep a hold on power."[26]

It goes even further. For those with a conspiratorial mindset, all of this evidence isn't proof that ideological violence comes mostly from one group of people, but rather it's simply another indication that "elites" are covering something up.

Deep state false flag psyop conspiracy theory

One crucial rule in the social media age is: "Don't apologize."

But Elon Musk took it further. After the Texas shopping mall shooting, he and others doubled down on their erroneous belief that the killer could not possibly have been inspired by far-right propaganda.

The Twitter boss later accused Bellingcat of being a "psychological operation"[27] – a term that might sound odd to anyone who's not fluent in conspiracy, but one that has become a core part of another crucial deflection technique.

A false flag is an attack that is carried out secretly, in order to pin responsibility on some other entity. A psyop – short for "psychological operation" – is an activity intended to change people's minds, often through propaganda and subterfuge. Both are real maneuvers that have been carried out in the real world, mostly in the context of military operations, and there are a number of historical examples of countries using false flag attacks as a pretext for war. Psychological operations are more varied, but standard examples include dropping propaganda leaflets on a country or playing constant loud music to a prisoner to try to break their will.

In the conspiracy world, however, a twisted reading of this real history has given rise to an idea that some now take as absolute truth: governments are in league with media, academia, and experts – not to mention legions of seemingly ordinary people who are really hired actors – to regularly stage violent attacks for propaganda purposes. In conspiracy world, false flags and psyops happen everywhere, all the time. They are the secret sauces that governments use to control their populations. And they are never exposed, except by the conspiracy theorists themselves, who have a preternatural ability to sniff them out.

The strategy was first widely popularized a decade ago by Alex Jones of Infowars – whom I'll discuss in greater detail later. Jones called the Sandy Hook massacre "synthetic, completely fake with actors, in my view, manufactured." It was a fiction – repeated a number of times in various ways on his show – that heaped misery upon the grief of parents of murdered children, and would later land Jones with a $1.4 billion defamation judgment.[28]

Jones and others implied – and sometimes just outright said – that the government fakes massacres, or stages real ones, in order to advance the interests of a shadowy elite cabal. When it came to Sandy Hook, the conspiracists were afraid of gun control, which they argued would lead to government tyranny.

It was the moment that confirmed Jones' transformation from a bombastic, entertaining questioner – who counted among his audience a sizeable number of people who might have called themselves left-wing – to something much darker and more definitively of the far right.

But where did he get this crazy falsehood from?

In early 2017, just a few months after the election of Donald Trump and just before I visited Sandy Hook and spoke with some of the families of the victims of the massacre, I spent an uncomfortable three hours in the living room of a retired school official named Wolfgang Halbig.

Halbig was a portly man with mottled skin and wire-frame glasses who lived in a large, yellow cookie-cutter house several miles into a gated subdivision in the middle of Florida. He had appeared several times on Infowars promoting the "false flag" claims.

"I call it an illusion. The biggest government illusion that's ever been pulled off by [the US Department of] Homeland Security," he told me.[29]

"I'll be honest with you," he said, "if I'm wrong, I need to be institutionalized." He told me that the plan was at least two years in the making and involved hundreds of "crisis actors."

This is the idea – popularized by Halbig, Jones and other Sandy Hook conspiracy theorists – that people are paid to fake massacres or violent protests. It's true that sometimes agencies and companies hire actors as part of training scenarios. But the conspiracy world meaning of the term is something wholly different.

Twitter is awash with dubious screenshots of job advertisements luring cash-strapped people into crisis actor work. The photos are usually Photoshopped, or junk generated by job board algorithms,[30] but they can fool people who don't think twice about why supposedly super-secret government operations would be openly advertised.

And somehow, despite Halbig's insistence that literally hundreds of people were involved, not one supposed "crisis actor" ever stepped forward to blow the whistle themselves. Like *2000 Mules*, the enormous scale of the conspiracy was in sharp contrast to the paucity of first-hand witnesses.

Halbig was a sad character, who would eventually face criminal charges and bankruptcy, and although Jones strapped rocket boosters to his speculative theories, which took off in a feverish way, his assertions were wholly untrue.

The underlying premise of the "psyop" idea – the notion that mass shootings and attacks move the needle of public opinion in America – has little evidence to support it. The impact of Sandy Hook on public attitudes on guns was mixed.[31] A federal assault weapons ban failed miserably, voted down by Republican senators along with a sizable chunk of Democrats. President Obama enacted a few administrative changes – such as instructing federal agencies to share data for gun owner background checks and allowing doctors to ask patients whether they had guns at home within the reach of children. Connecticut and some other states banned assault weapons. None of the tinkering stemmed gun ownership or gun deaths, both of which are significantly higher ten years later.[32] It wasn't a "psyop," but if it had been, it clearly hadn't worked, and any master manipulator would have ditched the tactic immediately.

That fact has not gone wholly unnoticed among the conspiratorial fringes. And so, over time, the supposed motivations for murderous plots have shifted from concrete attempts to pass legislation to more nebulous ideas. Today's mass shootings, conspiracists argue, are staged because the deep state wants to instill fear or control your mind, slur right-wing movements or prop up repressive conspiratorial movements, rather than, for instance, pass Senate Bill 150.

The dark brilliance of this adaptive strategy is that it can be used by the conspiracy fringes in countless ways and applied to all sorts of events, to great benefit in a world where social media attention can be turned into money and clout.

In May 2023, a 19-year-old man flew from St. Louis to Washington, DC, rented a truck, and crashed it into a barrier near the White House.[33] He took a Nazi flag from the back of the truck and later told an agent his goal was to "seize power, and be put in charge of the nation."[34] Nazis, he told investigators, have a "great history," and Hitler was a "strong leader." Clearly the suspect was under the sway of far-right ideology and quite possibly mental illness.

But conspiracists saw something altogether different.

"The U-Haul truck that 'crashed' outside of the White House tonight was conveniently carrying a 'Nazi flag,'" one tweeted. "The PSYOP is way too obvious these days."[35] What the possible "deep state" motive might have been for staging a minor news event was not made clear.[36]

It's impossible to tell exactly how someone like Elon Musk got the idea that Bellingcat, an open-source investigative outlet staffed by serious journalists and researchers, was somehow part of a nefarious deep state plot to change public opinion.[37] Bellingcat has received funding from government and international organizations, which is enough to give it a "psyop" stamp in some conspiracist circles. But there was absolutely no evidence that the facts of the Texas case were manipulated for some unspecified globalist goal. It seems most likely that Musk absorbed such bizarre and unevidenced ideas by paying attention to far-right activists on his own social network.

In fact, these deflection techniques have become so common in these online circles and are now such an ingrained technique on the conspiratorial far right that they are trotted out automatically on social networks, both mainstream and fringe, after every news story about a racially motivated mass killing.

In August 2023, a white man in his twenties went into a store in Jacksonville, Florida and shot dead three black people. The response from the authorities was swift – the perpetrator had left three documents on his computer and had told his father about them. The father contacted the police. The local sheriff held a press conference the same day, saying: "This shooting was racially motivated, and he hated black people."[38]

The conspiracy theorists thought they knew better.

"False flag operation," one X/Twitter user said. 4chan users on the racist /pol/ board, the hub of the alt-right, argued over whether the attack was faked by the government or not, at the same time discussing how "successful" it had been.

And in an attempt at false equivalence, far-right and conservative influencers pushed a convoluted conspiratorial narrative to try to equate the Jacksonville shooting with a previous slaughter: a school shooting in Nashville, Tennessee in March 2023. That horrific crime had been carried out by a transgender person who killed three children and three adults, and then was shot dead by police. Far-right activists seized on the suspect's declared identity and early reports that the killer had written a "manifesto" – later described as a rambling set of journals rather than a cohesive statement[39] – to insinuate that the killer was driven to kill by confusion over their gender identity. Conservatives demanded the release of the documents, against the wishes of most of the families of the parents at the school.[40]

In the hours after the Jacksonville killings, this same cohort misinterpreted the sheriff's remarks – perhaps deliberately – and claimed that the perpetrator's writings had been instantly released to the public.

That hadn't happened. In fact, when my colleagues and I began searching for the Jacksonville documents in the internet's darkest corners, we did not find them. Unlike the writings of the Buffalo and Texas killers, they were impossible to find – not circulating at all in public forums, even the obscure ones where far-right manifestos tend to end up. They weren't to be found, it later emerged, because although they were examined by police, they were never put online.

"Anyone else notice how we got the Jacksonville shooter's manifesto within hours of the 'racially motivated' incident, but we still don't have the Nashville Trans Terrorist's manifesto 5 months after they murdered Christian schoolchildren?" wrote far-right influencer DC Draino, repeating the false claim.[41]

He divined a political motive: "It's a simple explanation: One boosts the regime's racially divisive narrative. The other doesn't."

43

"It took 5 minutes to get the manifesto and motivation from the Jacksonville killer yet 5 months later and we still don't have the manifesto from the [Nashville] killer. Both were awful people but it appears one ideology doesn't align with the media narrative," tweeted another activist.[42]

When small portions of the Nashville murderer's writings did leak[43] to right-wing podcaster Stephen Crowder in late 2023, they included angry, violent language directed at white, wealthy people and a gay slur. Muddling the picture – though not for the ideologues who insisted that "leftist ideology" was to blame – were the facts that the killer was white, had attended the private school that they attacked, and among the victims was an African-American janitor.

The tactics of excuse, deflection and denial work to prevent any real reckoning on the broader right of American politics to examine the causes of extremist violence and to purge extremists from their ranks. They freeze out attempts to prevent violent ideology from marching further into the mainstream. To condemn murders or to point to evidence collected by law enforcement or the opinions of authorities, even the Trump-appointed director of US Homeland Security – who wrote in October 2020: "I am particularly concerned about white supremacist violent extremists who have been exceptionally lethal in their abhorrent, targeted attacks in recent years"[44] – is to be a traitor to the cause, a "cuck" or a sell-out.

Whoever's to blame for the killing, the conspiracists say, it's not people like them.

The rhetorical strategies I've outlined aren't limited to mass murders. Like those who were primed to believe in voter fraud, and thus were convinced by movies like *2000 Mules*, the idea of deep state manipulation and evil left-wing (or liberal, or antifa, or "mainstream media") malfeasance could be applied to all sorts of situations, in defiance of all kinds of logic. Once you buy into the ideas of mirror world, anything is possible.

The summer of 2023 was the hottest on record. Wildfires from Canada's worst-ever fire season forced thousands from their homes and repeatedly blanketed huge swathes of North America with smoke. The cloud, smelling of wood cooking and camping, lingered in the air even over my home in Chicago, signaling not relaxed vacation vibes, but something very, very wrong.

Far-right activists noticed that face masks were making a comeback, and some whipped up their supporters by prophesizing about the return of lockdowns. The more general prospect of a "climate lockdown" – government-imposed movement restrictions to limit fossil fuel consumption – had gained steam after Covid lockdowns ended and conspiracy influencers lost one of their key rallying points. Others cast suspicion on the causes of the fires or speculated that they had been deliberately started for one political reason or another.

Then in August, devastating fires hit the Hawaiian island of Maui, nearly totally destroying the town of Lahaina. The conspiracists went to work dreaming up deep state reasons for the devastation. It took a few days for solid ideas to crystallize, but once they did, they tore through fringe communities online.

One of the strangest theories was also one of the most popular: some speculated that the government or some other shadowy entity had deployed a "directed energy weapon." The proof, some said, was that some trees remained unburnt and that the fire left all the very richest people's homes unscathed. The first statement was true and explained by biology, while the second seemed true, but in fact was not.[45]

Through insinuation and "asking questions," influencers accused Maui's "woke billionaires" – Barack Obama, Bill Gates, Oprah, Jeff Bezos – of conspiring to start the fires as part of a plot to grab some of the world's prettiest and most valuable real estate. It didn't matter to the conspiracists that some of the celebrities mentioned weren't billionaires or didn't own property on Maui. And it was perhaps telling who was left off the list – Maui landowners (and confirmed billionaires) such as Larry Ellison and Peter Thiel. Ellison and Thiel, of course, also did not plot to steal land by starting wildfires. But they are notable supporters of right-wing causes and the Republican Party. Ellison even participated in a conference call about strategies to overturn the 2020 election, along with a representative of True The Vote, the election denial group that featured in *2000 Mules*.[46]

The Maui wildfire conspiracy theories[47] hewed to the ideas that had been developed in the wake of hate-motivated mass murders. Isolated facts were strung together to create a seemingly plausible narrative, a secret underground story that only the conspiracists were privy to. They were combined with criticism of the mainstream media, whom they accused of either downplaying the damage or failing to broadcast every batshit crazy theory that went viral, or of being bought off when some did look further and found nothing factual to back them up.

Researchers traced some of the spread of the conspiracy theories to foreign governments – China and Russia.[48] Like the "fake news" stories that circulated during the 2016 presidential election, the false information was not invented by foreign governments, but spread by elements who saw their divisive potential.

Most of all, the conspiracy theories were an attempt to distract and deny. Among the vast majority of the far right, man-made climate change is a truth that dare not be mentioned. They believe it is a hoax. And so, just as another cause must be found to explain far-right violence, it must be the deep state, or land-grabbing billionaires, rather than humanity's use of fossil fuels, that must be blamed for extreme weather events.

This is how conspiracy theories can work against even baby steps towards solutions to the most pressing problems facing the United States today. Gun violence, climate change, crime, immigration, racism, the decline of public morals – all of these issues feature high on lists of Americans' most pressing concerns.[49] Conspiracy thinking stops any meaningful attempts at solutions, however – substituting the prospect of change with endless secrets, and a revelation that is always just around the corner but never seems to quite arrive.

The conspiratorial excuses for violence and the twisted logic attached to them are huge and consequential ideas, more macabre and possibly even more damaging to the social fabric than election denial.

They provide a ready-made cover and deflection for even the worst forms of violence. But they only begin to touch the outer limits of outlandishness.

To truly gauge how far conspiracy thinking has advanced in American society – and how much it's burrowed into the mainstream – we have to examine an idea that has been called "the grand unified theory" of conspiracies.[50]

It is another concept that is rarely encountered in polite liberal American society – or if it is, it is whispered about as a shameful secret: *You'll never believe what my aunt thinks*. Not only is this particular cult utterly wild, its continued influence is even more baffling than the already implausible theories I've covered so far. Although its main outlets and proponents mostly disappeared into internet thin air years ago, and it's rarely even talked about by name these days, its tenets are more virulent than ever, and its activists have found their way into organizations and movements across the MAGA universe.

Make no mistake: QAnon is not yet dead.

4

QAnon lives on and on

He had a beard instead of face paint; a black shirt instead of no shirt. But the QAnon Shaman was unmistakable.

Jake Angeli appeared on my screen for a video call in June 2023, a few months after he finished his prison sentence for obstructing an official proceeding during the Capitol riot.

Angeli – dressed in furs and horns, wearing red, white and blue face paint, and hoisting an American flag – was the face of unrest on January 6, 2021. You've seen the pictures. He was a frequent attendee of prior pro-Trump and QAnon rallies, and on that day, Angeli was one of the first few dozen rioters into the Capitol. He entered the Senate chamber and sat down on the seat reserved for the vice president.

"Mike Pence is a fucking traitor," he snarled. He scribbled a message: "IT'S ONLY A MATTER OF TIME JUSTICE IS COMING!"[1]

Fortunately, the QAnon Shaman on my computer screen took an altogether different tone to start our conversation. It was his first interview with a mainstream media outlet since leaving prison.

"All of America, all the world is my tribe," he told me. "I feel a certain level of profound responsibility to humanity and to the planet Earth itself, the environment, the plants, animals, insects, the fungi."

I had a long list of questions for him. First of all: did he have any regrets?

"I do all I can to live without regrets, Mike," he said. "Regrets only weigh down the mind."

It was a curious turnaround. In November 2021, Angeli told a federal judge: "I am truly, truly repentant for my actions, because repentance is not just saying you're sorry. Repentance is apologizing and then moving in the exact opposite direction of the sin that you committed."

The judge called his *mea culpa* "the most remarkable I've heard in 34 years" on the bench, while handing him 41 months in prison, at the lower end of the sentencing guidelines.[2]

But now, as we spoke less than two years later, Angeli was regretting his regret. And he was clearly still heavily into the wild theories of QAnon. He denounced his former lawyer, who he claimed had made things up in a misguided attempt to get him a lighter sentence.

"I never said I was duped by Trump," he said, refuting an argument that had come up at his court hearing. "I never denounced Q or the QAnon community ... and I am not schizophrenic, bipolar, depressed or delusional."

Solitary confinement had been "a form of soft torture," he said, which had driven him to plead guilty and apologize. But although he contended he'd been entirely let down by the legal system, he still trusted it enough to appeal. He wanted his plea to be vacated.[3]

Angeli told me he believed QAnon itself was a "psyop," and introduced me to another meaning of that term. He didn't mean it in the normal pejorative far-right sense of a government operation designed to manipulate the sheeple. Instead, he saw it as a positive thing – sort of like a primal howl of the anti-deep state.

"It's a psychological operation that is intending to disseminate top secret information to people in our country so that we can understand the true intricacies of what is actually going on in our country and what has been going on for a long time as it relates to debt-based currency, things like child and human slavery or trafficking, blackmail and pedophilia rings," he told me.

Angeli went on to describe hidden sources of limitless energy and cures for cancer, discoveries buried by successive governments for decades. There was Operation Mockingbird – a real CIA public manipulation campaign that, in the view of conspiracists, had swelled to become an all-encompassing manipulative psyop total war on an unsuspecting public. QAnon was a corrective campaign launched by positive forces. At least, according to Angeli.

Although he no longer regretted his actions during the riot, he did admit he would have done one thing differently. In between marching around the Senate chamber and leaving notes for the vice president, he said he would have tried to stop some of the violence and destruction.

"I really tried to stop people from going crazy," he told me. "I would have tried a lot harder had I known what was going to happen.

"But who's going listen to the crazy guy in the face paint and the horns telling everybody to calm down?"[4]

QAnon began in 2017 in the ashes of that other conspiracy theory obsessed with elite power and pedophilia, Pizzagate.

Egged on by amateur detectives with hyperactive imaginations who read way too much into the leaked emails of Hillary Clinton aide John Podesta, Pizzagaters became obsessed with a Washington pizza joint called Comet Ping Pong, believing it to be the center of a child sex abuse ring run by leading Democrats. The theory reached such a fever pitch that a man from North Carolina stormed into Comet Ping Pong with a gun, shot out a lock, "investigated" – and found nothing.

QAnon, by contrast, was much more flexible, veering towards what logicians call "non-falsifiable." It was predicated on a series of cryptic communications on far-right message boards in 2017 and spawned an entire online subculture of Qdrops and crumbs (the messages themselves), bakers (fans interpreting the clues), reams of numerology, and melodramatic catchphrases like "The storm is coming" and "Where we go one, we go all."

While there was an actual human "Q" – most likely several people, including Jim and Ron Watkins, father and son who ran the 8chan message board – much, much more important than the leader was the group dynamic. QAnon's open-source nature made everyone a participant, contributing their own interpretations, hastily googled nuggets of information and YouTube videos and much more. It made for a sprawling, immersive, addictive conspiracy theory, complete with dissent, rivalries and intense discussions, giving the illusion of vigorous debate and political discourse, albeit entirely contained within the conspiracy community itself. Anything that wasn't considered part of the establishment or "deep state" was considered possibly true.

My colleagues and I developed a convenient shorthand definition for the movement: "A wide-ranging, completely unfounded theory that says that President Trump is waging a secret war against elite Satan-worshipping pedophiles in government, business and the media."

The pedophilia theme was the key. QAnon believers think they are saving children from evil. And if you think that, you'll probably be willing to do just about anything for your cause.

QAnon remained on the fringes until, in summer of 2018, it had something of a coming-out party. Supporters descended on a Trump rally in Florida and held up signs with QAnon slogans and websites. From there it steadily encroached into the mainstream and pulled in supporters from around the United States – and around the world. As QAnon gathered momentum, so did my efforts to find out more about who these people were and what they believed. And for a relatively brief period after that rally, this extremely online phenomenon could be observed out in the real world.

Scranton, Pennsylvania is only a couple of hours from America's east coast, but about halfway into the two-hour drive from Newark Airport, it feels like you're well into so-called "flyover" country. Fast-food outlets line the interstate, and Wal-Marts and Targets occasionally emerge from the valleys of the Poconos.

Scranton and its surroundings are a good example of the cultural divides that have transformed American politics. Rural areas outside the city are where you'll tend to find older voters and more Trump supporters. The city itself still leans Democrat. It has its polished parts and its shabby sections, and is currently best known to outsiders for two things – being the setting for the US version of *The Office*, and the birthplace of Joe Biden.

When I visited on the Fourth of July weekend in 2019, I found a quiet, positively peaceful town, barely roused by the fireworks crackling through the evening sky. American flags were plastered everywhere, including on a large truck parked opposite the city's grandest building – an old neoclassical railway station which has been turned into a luxury hotel.

A closer look, though, revealed that this was not just another generic patriotic display. As I inched closer to the truck, I noticed QAnon slogans on the side, a Photoshopped picture of Hillary Clinton in jail, an exhortation to "Save the children!" and another one demanding that Barack Obama be forced to reveal his "real" birth certificate. I would later find out that it was one of a small fleet of vehicles owned by a local businessman who made them a frequent sight on the streets of Scranton.

The grand hotel itself was the venue for the latest stop on something called the "We Love Trump Keep America Great Tour." It was billed as an unofficial gathering of the president's supporters, but what drew me here were the headline speakers – including several key influencers in the world of QAnon.

I interviewed one of them just before he went on stage. Dylan Wheeler, a lanky, tall, blonde Midwesterner in his twenties, was traveling the country making the most of his recent internet fame. Hundreds of thousands followed his Twitter account, @EducatingLiberals, which sprinkled in red meat conservative slogans with QAnon content.

"QAnon cares about justice for humanity," Dylan told me. "You have to understand that the globalists with all the money in this world, the Rothschilds who have half of the world's wealth ... they have agendas. They have a plan for a New World Order and they want to put a one-world government in place."

He seemed completely self-possessed and untroubled as he said this, as if he were weighing up the merits of the Minnesota Twins roster or describing the house band at a local bar. I swallowed hard and tried to offer up some questions that would make at least a little bit of sense to people listening back on Planet Reality.

"You think QAnon's a conspiracy against Donald Trump?" I asked.

"No! If anything it's a military intelligence operation that almost selected Donald Trump, that's been in the making since JFK died when he wanted to take down the Federal Reserve because the Federal Reserve is not backed by gold. We're basically slaves to the money," he said.

"Um."

"It's a lot to digest," he acknowledged.

We went inside, and Dylan made his pitch to crowd. The other speakers included Scott Pressler, an anti-Islam activist and repeat guest on conservative talk shows, including one hosted by Steve Bannon, the former Breitbart editor and key Trump advisor. Pressler forged a career as a Republican hype man; he would later travel to Washington on January 6, 2021, although he did not go inside the Capitol. Another star of the Q universe, former celebrity journalist Liz Crokin, was scratched as a speaker at the last minute. Crokin's mainstream career had ended after she suffered a bout of meningitis and brain damage due to a sexually transmitted disease,[5] but she had since reinvented herself as a champion of Pizzagate and QAnon.

A contingent came from a local group called Women for Trump – dressed in pink along with red, white and blue, they were the forerunners of the Moms for Liberty group that would become a political force just a few years later. But a promised platoon of Bikers for Trump never showed, and the overall turnout was small – maybe 100 people at most, who half-filled a cavernous room meant for lavish weddings and corporate awards ceremonies.

Despite the disappointing crowd size, QAnon's true potential was on display. The crowd weren't slavish fans. They hadn't turned out to hear about Qdrops and breadcrumb trails and bakers and all the other assorted QAnon lore that would later be picked over in news reports and queried by baffled editors. Instead, the people in that room were retirees and moms, small business owners and Trump supporters in red shirts which neatly matched their MAGA hats. Few appeared younger than 50, and more than a few were grandmothers.

"I've heard of Q," one told me. "It's not like it's been portrayed in the media. You should look into it."

"I don't agree with everything Q says," said a Women for Trump member, "but he has some valid points."

The crowd in Scranton was more about the vibe than the specifics. They couldn't identify any particular crime or victim, and nor could I find anyone who admitted that they fully believed there was an organized satanic child abuse ring operating at the highest levels of government. These were not the young male basement dwellers of 4chan, but the QAnon message resonated with them.

They were convinced that children were in danger, that there were threats coming at them from every direction, and they were looking for someone to fight back. They were living through an age of mass school shootings and skyrocketing mental health problems, a confusing terrain of social media bullying and new and strange ideas that would soon be called "woke." Several mentioned immigration and their detailed knowledge about what was supposedly happening on the southern border, which was about 2,000 miles away.

Democrats were evil, they thought, children were in danger, there was corruption at the top, their country was in mortal peril, only Trump could root it out. They were the mainstream, and they didn't really see much of a difference between QAnon and MAGA.

As the years progressed, this version of QAnon – rather than the numerology, the cryptic messages and robotic slogans – would persist, be watered down further, and would soak completely into the mainstream American right.

And as it did so, QAnon vibes – rather than its bizarre specifics – would become one of the paranoid cornerstones of the far-right. It would gain the potential to motivate millions, not just the small crowd that turned out to listen to Dylan Wheeler speak in Scranton.

A couple of people at the Scranton gathering later ran for public office and, like Pressler, demonstrated the links between the far-right, QAnon-tinged fringes and the mainstream of the Republican Party. Lauren Witzke was a former drug addict who had gotten clean and found religion. As one of the event organizers, she was cordial, professionally dressed, and helpful to the assembled media, which consisted of me, my video journalist colleague, and nobody else.

Witzke later won the Republican Party nomination for US Senate in Delaware and further spread bizarre conspiracy theories[6] before losing by a wide margin. Another man, Michael Sisco, had driven a few hours from Maryland with a group of people in their twenties and thirties. He told me he was a "traditional reactionary" and specifically, a "monarchist." I put to him that the other traditional reactionaries in the room might balk at being ruled by a king. He was nonplussed.

"What if you told them, 'President Trump for life'?" Sisco suggested. "They might get excited." He too would later try his hand at running for office.[7]

I left Scranton the next day with an interesting but bizarre story. I wouldn't have bet on any continued influence of QAnon on the wider conservative movement. Even the speakers had pulled their punches. Dylan Wheeler made veiled references to criminality, but despite being in a safe space, didn't straight-up accuse top Democrats of being part of a massive pedophile ring.

It had already been nearly a year since the movement really captured mainstream attention,[8] but it looked like it would continue to be confined to the margins.

Of course, that's not how it turned out at all.

The riot of January 6 which landed Angeli in prison also marked the end of QAnon's first act.

It seems remarkable that someone so devoted to the inner workings of the "deep state" had nothing much to say after the events of January 6, but the speculation is that those behind the Q messages suddenly became very concerned about their role in whipping up the crowd and the potential prosecution that could result. Q occasionally sent out other cryptic missives, but the momentum was gone – a brief reemergence around the time of the 2022 midterm elections went largely ignored.[9]

It didn't really matter. The idea had been planted and the panic was in full flow, now boosted not by hardcore believers, but by the type of people who join organizations like Women for Trump. Some followers, like Angeli, remained in the grip of the fringe ideas that QAnon had ignited. Others, like Wheeler, turned the other way. He later told me he had lost faith in Q, and his social media posts indicated he was increasingly concerned with the shape of the earth (which, he contended, was flat).

But many, many more bought into the general themes of QAnon. I noticed them in some surprising places. In Montana, I walked out of a café only to be stopped short by the window of a barber shop across the street. It had a giant letter Q and the acronym WWG1WGA ("Where we go one, we go all") plastered on it. And watered-down versions of QAnon ideas were starting to seep into popular culture – not just through memes or YouTube videos or barbershop windows, but through mainstream entertainments.

In the summer of 2023, the independent film *Sound of Freedom* was a surprise hit – one of the highest-grossing films of the year. The movie depicts the fictionalized story of Tim Ballard, a former CIA and Department of Homeland Security official who founded Operation Underground Railroad, which helps sex trafficking victims. Ballard's methods have been controversial, and he resigned his post with the organization after allegations of sexual misconduct.[10] Ballard has denied being a QAnon supporter, but he did see the energy of the movement as a positive, once commenting: "Some of these theories have allowed people to open their eyes ... So now it's our job to flood the space with real information so the facts can be shared."[11]

Ballard was depicted in the film by Jim Caviezel, the actor who is perhaps best known for playing Jesus in *The Passion of the Christ*. Caviezel had a more straightforward take on QAnon; he believed some of its theories. He repeated baseless Q theories about elite pedophiles sucking adrenochrome out of children[12] and spoke in front of a QAnon convention in Las Vegas.[13]

Sound of Freedom itself was not a deliberate QAnon vehicle, and many in its audience – perhaps the vast majority – were not believers. But the film provided a springboard for the conspiracy theory's core ideas about the ever-present threat of child sex trafficking rings.

Largely because of QAnon, the fear of a dangerous secret cabals of elites preying on children, which has persisted in the background for centuries, was given new focus and new status in the American political scene. It was now common to see protesters at rallies who wore T-shirts which, for instance, alluded to a popular QAnon video which purported to show Joe Biden sniffing a child. There was something nefarious going on, they were sure of it. The subtext was not very sub: they appeared to believe the president is a pedophile. And if the evil extended to the top, there was no stopping it without violent, dramatic action.

QAnon was emblematic of the paranoia that has overwhelmed the fringes of the right. And when Q disappeared, the energy that propelled the movement needed somewhere to go. Believers were focused on the elites, billionaires, Democrats, Joe Biden and George Soros – but needed still more scapegoats, new enemies to target. And so, buoyed by larger culture war trends, gay people and trans people became the focus of a new backlash.

5

Proud Boys and "groomers"

In September 2023, the day after Labor Day, I arrived at the US District Court in Washington, DC for the sentencing of the leader of the Proud Boys.

Enrique Tarrio repeatedly led his group through the streets of Washington in the weeks leading up to the Capitol riot, which was not an isolated event, but the culmination of a series of protests, rallies and brawls. No other street-level organization was as deeply involved in the ongoing effort to keep Donald Trump in power. Proud Boys, including Tarrio himself,[1] had been stabbed during several of the gatherings. By January 6, 2021, they were losing faith in law enforcement to protect them and losing hope that Trump would remain in the White House. Paranoia was more than creeping in – it was overwhelming.

Although he wasn't in Washington on January 6, 2021 – he'd been ordered out of the city after being arrested for burning a Black Lives Matter flag and on weapons charges – Tarrio cheered on his boys from a hotel room in nearby Baltimore.

"Proud of my Boys and my country," he wrote on the social network Parler.[2] "Don't fucking leave."

After the riot, he had bullishly defended his comrades. But in court, dressed in a prison-issue orange jumpsuit, with a full beard, his head shaved, he struck an apologetic tone.

"I failed," he told the judge. "I failed miserably. I thought myself morally above others, and this trial has shown me how wrong I was to believe this."

He apologized to the police officers who were at the Capitol that day, and to the residents of Washington.

"What happened on January 6th was a national embarrassment," he said.

He acknowledged that Donald Trump had lost the 2020 presidential election and admitted that he had suspicions that this was the case well before the riot, but facing the censure of his closest friends and allies, he had continued on the path of attempted revolution.

"I am not a political zealot. Inflicting harm or changing the results of the election was not my goal. I didn't think it was even possible to change the results of the election," he said. "When I get home, I want nothing to do with politics, groups, activism or rallies."

The judge acknowledged Tarrio's words, but noted that they fell short of true contrition. Tarrio hadn't quite apologized for his actions that day, he said. The former leader of the Proud Boys had sort of missed the point.

"The jury did not convict Mr. Tarrio for engaging in politics," the judge said, "they convicted him for seditious conspiracy."

He sentenced Tarrio to 22 years in prison, the longest term given to anyone involved in the riot.

Like the persistence of QAnon ideas, the survival of the Proud Boys is a remarkable fact and a testament to the continued relevance of militant far-right ideas in American politics. Tarrio and other leaders ended up in jail in part on evidence provided by former members who testified against them. The group was booted off social media. The group led by Stewart Rhodes, the Oath Keepers, almost entirely dissolved after the riot.

But somehow local Proud Boys chapters around the country soon found themselves strangely in sync with the mainstream of American conservative life and with a renewed purpose: action against transgender and gay people.

There were several notable actions. At one of them, in March 2023, Proud Boys joined a protest against a drag story hour in Manhattan's West Village. Counter-protesters showed up, and the scene turned ugly. There was yelling, shoving, brawling and an arrest.[3]

One sign held up by a protester seemed to encapsulate the crowd's objections. It called drag queen story hours "the greatest grooming program ever devised." A T-shirt made a QAnon reference.[4] Another protester was certain of what was going on inside the building, claiming that people inside were "trying to indoctrinate [children] into trangenderism."[5]

It was an idea plucked straight from the QAnon people. Children were being corrupted by evil adults. They were in grave danger of sexual assault, and a broad coalition of government officials, media workers and left-wing activists were conspiring to "normalize" underage sexual activity. And the time was perfectly ripe for the marriage of conspiratorial thinking and gender panic.

Politics on the right had moved on from 2016, when Donald Trump famously said that transgender people should be able to use whatever bathroom they want.[6]

Arguments about gender and trans rights now roil all sorts of people in societies all around the world, and debates do not always break along traditional political lines. The pandemic cast new attention on our responsibilities towards children. Even though the vast majority aren't at risk of serious harm from the virus, the measures some adults imposed – the closing of schools, social distancing and the closing off of social life – had profound impacts on the very youngest. Far-right activists stepped into the pool of anxieties around children with a scapegoat – trans activists and their "elite" supporters.

These fears spread far and wide, and well beyond traditional right-wing activists. There were arguments about yanking books with sexual content out of school libraries – trumping any focus on free speech with the idea of "parental rights," a novel notion being tested in various ways around the country, which says that parents are entitled to a veto over any public school policy, rule or portion of the curriculum that they personally disagree with.

But the main thrust, and one that fringe activists knew could get wider traction, was against trans people. It cropped up in some strange ways. Big companies faced boycotts – including Anheuser-Busch for fleetingly associating its Bud Light brand with a transgender influencer, and retail outlet Target for selling a Pride Month range including items such as swimsuits for transgender people.[7]

Driving the drama and spurring people to action were a number of far-right podcasters and social media personalities who were willing to portray transgender rights and "inclusivity" capitalism as a profound sexual and mortal threat to children.

Dozens of anti-drag protests were recorded every month in the US, according to the Institute for Strategic Dialogue, and those numbers were on the increase through early 2023.

Crucially, researchers noted, the protesters consisted not just of "traditional anti-LGBTQ+ groups but include growing numbers of assorted other actors, from local extremists and white supremacists through to parents' rights activists, members of anti-vaxxer groups, and Christian nationalists."

The researchers noted that while public debate about what constitutes appropriate entertainment for children is "absolutely legitimate," the protests and other actions "only serve to undermine that discussion, with chilling consequences for free expression, and create fertile ground for a potential uptick in violence."[8]

One group, they found, was the most active on the anti-drag protest scene: the Proud Boys.

It was a curious development because, perhaps surprisingly, it was a departure for the group.

On a chilly night early in 2019, I met Edie Dixon at a gathering of Proud Boys in Vancouver, Washington State, a suburb of Portland. We were interviewing Proud Boys and filming as they went about their favorite social activities, drinking and smoking as they drifted in and out of a neighborhood bar.

Dixon was not a member of the group – she was transgender, and thus not eligible for membership. But she called herself a spokesperson and facilitated our entrée into the local chapter. The Proud Boys not only seemed to know her, but regarded her as an entertaining asset rather than a disruptive presence, and certainly as a friend rather than an enemy. She floated around, posed for pictures, and told us of the boys, proud and otherwise, that she had dated.

The Proud Boys were eager to show a visiting journalist their more accepting side. In the Vancouver group there were gay members and even – gasp – a Democrat. They wanted to prove they were more tolerant than their mortal enemies in Portland: committed anti-fascists. The two groups fought numerous battles throughout the Trump years, battles which would soon intensify and become more frequent. In 2020, after the murder of George Floyd, the city would see night after night of violence, an orgy of brutal political street fighting unparalleled in recent American history.

As the Proud Boys approached max drunk and the night started to wind down, we agreed to give Dixon a lift back into the city. She told us that Portland's left-wing establishment was evil and brainwashed, she'd received much more hate coming out as a Trump supporter in Portland than she had coming out as trans among her conservative friends. She said that the Proud Boys were misunderstood, more than that, they were persecuted and unsafe on the streets of Portland, and it all stemmed from their support of one man and an irrational reaction by the left.

"I just love Trump," she told us, adjusting her red MAGA hat.

Dixon told us that she had made real friends among the Proud Boys, that there was a real sense of community in the group, and that the only hate she'd encountered came from "the other side" – antifa.[9] She was less forthcoming about her application to a white nationalist organization and her anti-Semitic sympathies.[10]

Anti-trans and anti-gay sentiment has always been significant on the far right, but cracks in what used to be a pretty monolithically straight movement began to show during the rise of the alt-right. Some of the more "moderate" alt-right influencers were themselves gay or didn't think sexuality was a big deal. On the other hand, more extreme segments were definitely not cool with gay people, and many slurred them as "degenerates," an unsubtle term plucked directly from the language of Nazi Germany.[11]

Where the Proud Boys stand on many issues, including gender and sexuality, has varied over the years. The group has consistently, and quite deliberately, flummoxed outside observers. They called themselves a drinking club, but had a political orientation from the very start. They railed against political correctness and had libertarian values when it came to drugs and guns – but were angry defenders of traditional values and gender roles.

This calculated ideological ambiguity was a trap for critics who tried to lump them in with neo-Nazis, certain types of alt-right extremists and white supremacists. The extremism of the Proud Boys came not necessarily from their paleoconservative views, but from how they were prepared to back them up with violent action. They are far-right, but not necessarily or always white nationalist. Tarrio calls himself Afro-Cuban, and was certainly not the only ethnic minority member. They were shapeshifters, with rules and "degrees" of membership, but not holding too hard and fast to any particular ideology or set of instructions for living. Their structure provided more of a guttural feeling than a sense of purpose. They attracted men who wanted to feel, in a traditional sense, manly.

Experts studying the Proud Boys have rightfully pointed out to me that the group's dedication to tolerance was highly variable. Chapters in big cities on the coasts, even though part of the same far-right group, were more likely to lean in a bit on cosmopolitan values, while chapters in the Midwest and South could be less welcoming.

But for all their paleoconservative ideas about the place of men in the world, for the first few years of their existence the Proud Boys identified as hardcore libertarians. They swore they were the accepting ones; they weren't the kind of people who told other people what to do.

Three years after I spoke to Edie Dixon, the Proud Boys were no longer preaching a story of live-and-let-live. Instead, they focused their street-level activity on Pride events and drag story hours. Tolerance – or at least, lip service to tolerance – was gone.

To find out more, around the time of Tarrio's trial in early 2023, I contacted the group's founder, Gavin McInnes. I was slightly surprised when he called me back. When we were shooting our documentary in Portland, he not only refused to do an interview, but – before we had even shot a second of footage – the group's lawyer threatened to sue us.

But now, as his comrades faced lengthy jail sentences, he was the one sounding besieged.

"You're probably going to ask me about white supremacy and January 6th and the insurrection, and none of those are real," he complained.

His career was in tatters, he told me, and it wasn't his fault. He had told the Proud Boys – he was still very much a cheerleader for the group and in contact with its members – not to go to Washington on January 6. They ignored him, he said, just as the media ignored him when he said that the Proud Boys weren't a white supremacist group and racism hadn't been a part of American society for at least half a century.

"I think entering the Capitol was wrong," he said. "But I also think it's wrong to swear in front of your kids, it's wrong to drink more than a few beers and drive. I think it's wrong to insult your wife. These are all around the same thing."

He ticked off a list of standard excuses for the Capitol riot. The FBI knew it was going to happen, he said, and this was proven by the fact that a man named Ray Epps was involved, but never arrested (although, later, he was – and pleaded guilty to a crime[12]), left-wing protests weren't met with the same law enforcement response, and so on. He had a profound sense of grievance – he felt he and the Proud Boys were the victims. The federal government was taking fathers – some of whom were war heroes – away from their families. His fraternity was "the most misunderstood club in history."

Time and again on his podcast, McInnes railed against what he thought were false complaints made by feminists and ethnic minorities. They were snowflakes, with an exaggerated sense of grievance. But now he was convinced that he was the real victim, and that his Proud Boys were scapegoats.

I asked him about the Proud Boys protests at drag events. He had no problem with drag, he said – "it's funny, it's silly."

But he was convinced something new and nefarious was emerging.

"These drag queen story hours are bringing a sexual character to children. No one has a problem with gays reading to kids, some normal gay," he said. "These are essentially the gay version of strippers. And I would be outraged if strippers with thigh-high boots were reading to kids."

McInnes continued talking even as he became irritated by my follow-up questions and accused me of "virtue signaling." Given the recent uptick in general anger at LGBTQ events, I somehow doubted that most Proud Boys followed the nuances of McInnes' pro-drag, sort-of-pro-gay argument. But they definitely heard his conclusion.

"I'm not saying kids are going to get raped at the drag queen story hour. But under the auspices of 'gay is OK,' which of course it is, you're now getting sexual around kids ... I think there's a real normalization of kids and sexuality going on in America right now. And if there's one hill to die on, that's the hill."

The panic over transgender and gay people spread quickly throughout the right-wing fringes and soon became accepted wisdom among more mainstream right-wing audiences.

Those who viewed the world through this so-called "groomer" lens saw evidence of a dark plot everywhere they looked. At a New York City Pride parade, one or two marchers chanted "We're here, we're queer, we're coming for your children."[13] The clip was taken literally by a number of right-wing influencers.[14]

When Connecticut lawmakers made a tweak to the state's anti-discrimination law, a conservative group fretted that it would lead to pedophiles working in jobs where they had direct contact with children.[15] Peter Wolfgang of the Family Institute of Connecticut explained to me that under a particular reading of the new law, pedophilia could be considered a "protected characteristic." If the pedophile had never acted out on their desires and been convicted of a crime, and had publicly declared their perversion, theoretically they could sue if, for instance, they were turned down for a job as a school bus driver.

It was a theoretical legal argument that the sponsors of the bill told me was so odd that it had never once come up in legislative hearings. Of course, they said, they didn't want pedophiles working as school bus drivers. Who in their right mind would want that? But those on the conservative fringes, primed to see degeneracy everywhere, picked up the idea and ran with it. The law inspired blog posts and more QAnon-style invective on X/Twitter. One writer deduced that Democrats "are determined to normalize pedophilia"[16] and illustrated his post with a picture of drag queens.

The bill passed anyway. One lawmaker, Dominque Johnson, seemed slightly baffled at how a relatively straight-forward legislative exercise had been turned into a culture war battle.

"This is Connecticut," she told me. "People aren't really into extremes here."

And talk of "normalizing" pedophilia was definitely not limited to niche blogs, anonymous accounts or Connecticut. Tucker Carlson, after being removed from his slot as the country's most popular cable news host, rapidly descended into conspiracy and paranoia. He spent his second independently produced video thundering against what he saw as a hard march towards social acceptance of child sexual abuse.

"One by one our old taboos have been struck down," he told his viewers.[17] He rattled off a long list of things that supposedly had become acceptable: stealing, flaunting wealth, hitting women, smoking pot in public, accepting welfare payments.

"So it probably shouldn't surprise us that the greatest taboo of all is teetering on the edge of acceptability: child molestation."

Carlson wondered why the shooting of a convicted sex offender by vigilante Kyle Rittenhouse wasn't actively celebrated – although the shooting had to do with fractious Black Lives Matter protests, not with the man's crimes. He wondered why an investigation by the *Wall Street Journal* into child sexual abusers on Instagram hadn't received more attention, despite appearing on the front page of a leading newspaper and being repeated by numerous other news sites.[18]

Carlson plowed on. What the so-called mainstream media were focusing on instead of the supposed elite-driven project to normalize pedophilia were things like white nationalism and the Capitol riot. These were distractions, he said, from a devious social agenda. The gay trans lobby was coming for your children, and only those who were paying careful attention would be able to thwart it. Carlson[19] exhorted his audience to see, like he did, an existential battle.

"Cling to your taboos like your life depends on them, because it does. Cherish and protect them like family heirlooms. That's exactly what they are."

The video was popular – watched by more than 60 million people, at least by X/Twitter's count. Carlson, first through his Fox News show and now online, is one of the key – and certainly one of the most popular and mainstream – propagators of the style of dark and desperate paranoia which is now so prevalent on the right wing of American politics. His arguments were virtually indistinguishable from those of protesting Proud Boys and QAnon influencers.

Alongside election fraud and the panic over transgender people, there was another issue that had risen to become a far-right obsession with potentially huge mainstream crossover appeal. It was forged in the advanced stages of the Covid-19 pandemic, which itself spawned so many fantasies about politics and social control. Anti-vaccination views were once mostly associated with natural health, organic-eating yoga types, more affluent and left-leaning than most. Even in suburbs where "We believe in science" yard signs outnumbered Trump voters, many people likely knew a vaccine skeptic or someone who outright refused to get a shot.

But the pandemic, the anti-vaccination lobby and the American political backdrop all combined to shift and embolden the needle-haters. Hardcore anti-vaxxers are now one of the key nodes of America's pro-Trump far right.

6

Anti-vaccine derangement syndrome

In early January 2023, my family rushed home from an outing to Lincoln Park Zoo, picked up some pizzas and ensconced ourselves on the sofa just in time to watch our beloved Buffalo Bills kick off to the Cincinnati Bengals.

More than 23 million people tuned in to watch the most anticipated matchup of the National Football League season, a prime time battle between two of the league's best teams.[1]

Nobody was quite prepared for what happened next.

About nine minutes into the game, a Cincinnati player collided with Bills' defensive back Damar Hamlin. Hamlin got up for a second, then collapsed on the field. He had suffered a cardiac arrest, and nearly died. Medical teams performed CPR for what seemed like an eternity before rushing Hamlin to the hospital. The game was cancelled.

Most of those millions of people watching saw an unfortunate injury to a young man playing a brutal game. I retreated to my office. I knew that many thousands of others would see something completely different. Obsessed with a pseudoscientific theory, they would immediately link Hamlin's injury to Covid vaccines.

And indeed, within minutes came the flood:

Everybody knows what happened to Damar Hamlin because it's happened to too many athletes around the world since COVID vaccination was required in sports.[2]

This is a tragic and all too familiar sight right now: Athletes dropping suddenly.[3]

Prior to 2021, Athletes collapsing on the field was NOT a normal event. This is becoming an undeniable (and an extremely concerning) pattern. 💉💉 [4]

That last tweet, viewed at least 1.3 million times, came from an account promoting a film which had come out few months before. Although its evidence was arguably even less convincing than that of *2000 Mules*, *Died Suddenly* had crystallized anti-vaccine arguments, and was at the center of a new wave of anti-vaccine activism that had swept the far right. The film, and its social media presence, ensured that even though there was zero evidence that Hamlin's injury had anything to do with vaccination, millions would be enraged by the lie.

"Nice to meet you, Mike. I'm going to just change my tie," Stew Peters pointed at his chest. "They say I should be wearing a red tie instead."

Peters was prepared for us, with the exception of his neck-wear. His team had rented a unit in a small industrial complex in the coastal town of Vero Beach, Florida. Vero Beach is a place filled with palm trees, margarita-slinging bars and tourists in sandals – an oddly chill place to encounter one of the snarling stars of America's ferocious anti-vaccine movement and the man behind *Died Suddenly*.

Inside the unit, his own team had already set up cameras and lights. The crew included several of his relatives and Lauren Witzke, the Republican Senate nominee from Delaware who I had met among the QAnon believers in Scranton. Peters' team was going to record our team recording him.

"I'm an investigator," said Peters, a former bounty hunter and aspiring rapper, once all the cameras started rolling. "The kinds of criminals that we're dealing with now are killing millions of people, rather than just a one off here or there."

Although our encounter was civil at the start, Peters grew increasingly agitated as, over the course of about an hour, we brought up the evidentiary problems in his film.

Died Suddenly contained interviews with morticians, medical insiders, and clip after clip of people passing out, supposedly from the effects of Covid vaccines. The short video bursts were the first clue that something was up. Several dated from before the availability of vaccines against Covid. Others depicted people whose fainting spells were definitely caused by other things.

The movie also contained dramatic shots of blood clots. Some were taken from a training video which was shot before the emergence of Covid, much less Covid vaccines. Others had natural, non-Covid explanations. The movie also contained frightening statistics about fertility – which were easily debunked in a few seconds online.

It was dramatic, popular, terrifying propaganda, but its fans didn't really care. *Died Suddenly* built on the success of another Peters film, *Watch the Water* (the title echoed a QAnon slogan). *Watch the Water* posited that Covid symptoms were really caused by snake venom being pumped into the water supply.

Like *2000 Mules*, *Died Suddenly* was an excellent example of the conspiracy genre – a film that was able to draw in millions of fans because they were already predisposed to believe that vaccines were killing millions of people.

"I'm the only person out here telling the truth," Peters told us.

His conspiracy thinking did not stop with Covid. Not only was he convinced that the disease was a hoax, that vaccines were bioweapons and reporters were liars, but also that everyone in the mainstream media was covering up for pharmaceutical companies, the war in Ukraine was being faked, both major American political parties were colluding behind the scenes, homosexuality was unnatural and should be made illegal, and the moon landings never happened. I felt a small crumb of comfort at the last one on that list; old-school conspiracy theories seem quaint these days. But then he insisted that anyone involved in promoting Covid vaccines should be executed. I pressed him. Who did he consider eligible for the guillotine? Executives, politicians, scientists, journalists?

"All of you people, for sure," he said. "If you're found guilty of crimes against humanity and responsible for killing children, yes, that's very clear."

"So wait," I said. "We should be put to death?"

"Did you hear what I just said?" he snapped. "Stop trying to be hyperbolic. Just stop it! Are you guilty of crimes against humanity?"

The outburst was so bizarre I wanted to laugh, but managed to keep a straight face.

"I don't think so," I said.

"I guess that will be up to a tribunal to figure out," Peters continued. "A citizens' grand jury. That'll be up to a military tribunal, the Nuremberg hearings, to figure out whether you're guilty of crimes against humanity. That's not for me to decide."

Anti-immunization activists have been around for centuries – even before the invention of modern vaccines.[5] They're a group with an array of perspectives and concerns, which makes them difficult to accurately summarize. Some have a long distrust of mainstream medicine – including members of minority groups who have ample real-world evidence to back up such views.

But the group that's important for our purposes is one made up of hardcore activists. Aside from a flare-up around the turn of the century, following a wave of attention given to British doctor Andrew Wakefield, these highly engaged anti-vaxxers have generally been confined to the margins of health policy, and have rarely been a noteworthy far-right constituency. In fact, they've more often been associated with natural health types, yoga fans and others who are more often into left-wing ideas.

That's not necessarily the whole picture – there's ample evidence to suggest that those on the libertarian right have been just as vaccine skeptical as organic clean-living types.[6] But the response to Covid marked an inflection point in this dynamic. As the pandemic progressed, anti-vaccination sentiment became increasingly more mainstream on the right of American politics, where the anti-vax lobby found a receptive audience among those suspicious of elites, scientists and politicians. Anti-vaxxers on either end of the political spectrum began to start sounding more like each other than those closer to the political middle.

To fully explain how this happened, we need to back up to the time shortly before the pandemic broke out. At the start of 2020, I was one of the editors who gathered together a crew of journalists which eventually became the first pan-BBC News disinformation team. We had our eye on the US election later in the year until reports emerged from China of a disease caused by a novel virus. Even then, it was difficult to see what was coming. In February 2020, I was baffled by Los Angeles airport workers with masks on their faces. Six weeks later, Britain and most of the rest of the world went into lockdown.

A fascinating pattern developed over that intense and confusing first pandemic year. As the virus first began to spread, viral rumors and dubious forwarded chain messages made claims of huge secret death tolls and cover-ups of the true scale of death. New York's Central Park would be turned into a graveyard; or all doctors and nurses were being called into hospitals, which would be turned into fortresses; or authorities were commandeering ice rinks in order to store stacks of dead bodies.

The toll in those early days was, of course, enormous – an estimated half a million deaths worldwide by mid-June.[7] But by some measures that was less than expected, and certainly less than the worst projections and wildest rumors had anticipated. After the first huge viral wave, with emergency hospitals going unused but businesses and individuals facing a patchwork of rules and restrictions in many countries, new conspiracy narratives unfolded. The virus was not extraordinarily dangerous, but the opposite – completely benign or even fictional. This spawned whispers of secret plots to subjugate and control the population, supposedly using the pandemic as an excuse.

There was the idea that people were actually being killed not by the virus, but by 5G radio waves. Other theories said mask rules were a test of compliance, or that the whole pandemic was somehow "fake" – planned by authorities or allowed to happen. It was, as the title of one viral film filled with conspiracy theories[8] labeled it, a "plandemic," a scheduled and designed disease outbreak.

Who was doing the planning, what exactly their goals were, and how they were getting away with it varied widely from conspiracy community to social media interest group. But this haziness was seen by many as a strength rather than a weakness – proof that they, the conspiracists, were open-minded free thinkers, as opposed to just believing the "official" story being pushed by government and the "mainstream media," with its prosaic tales of a new virus causing a respiratory illness, and constant warnings to take uncomfortable evasive action, like donning masks, limiting social contact and restricting movement.

It's hard to quantify how many people really and truly bought into the theories and insinuations of the *Plandemic* film and the thousands of Facebook groups and micro-movements that sprung up spreading Coronavirus conspiracies. But their numbers were certainly in the millions. Many were drawn to the alternative theories in the first place – or found their conspiratorial thinking exacerbated – by the stress and economic upheaval that came in Covid's wake.

And it soon became clear that Covid posed a substantial mortal danger to certain segments of the population – the elderly and obese, those who are immunocompromised – but almost no risk of death to others, including healthy young adults and children. And yet working-age people and children were among the most affected by the closing of businesses, offices and schools.

Many decided they wanted no part of any collective effort to stop the disease. An unknown proportion of their number blew right by valid political and scientific arguments about the efficacy of lockdown and the complicated balance of risks into full-blown conspiracy territory.

Whenever I picture a typical anti-vaccination activist, my mind keeps returning to a marcher walking through central London at a lockdown protest in April 2021, just as restrictions in Britain were coming to an end, never to return again.

A crowd of tens of thousands marched through the city, the bulk of the throng taking about 15 or 20 minutes to march by a point near Oxford Circus, where our crew was stationed. Some marchers would later howl that hundreds of thousands or millions of people participated, and would share shots online of huge swarms, some of which had been taken from previous protests that had nothing to do with Covid lockdowns at all – in other words, fake photos used to try to bolster false theories.

I snapped pictures of the some of the biggest banners carried that day and many less prominent, handmade ones. One of the people I captured on my phone was a woman who looked in her thirties, wearing a blue sundress and sunglasses. She would not have looked out of place picking up a few bits and bobs from M&S on her way to a picnic in Hyde Park. Her sign read: "Aim your toxic syringe away from my grandpa. Keep your poisonous GMOs away from our food. Aim your godless 5G masts away from my baby's bedroom. I DO NOT CONSENT."

Other people we spoke to that day swore that the conspiracists were on the very fringes of their anti-lockdown movement, like extremist Islamists who pop up at pro-Palestine marches. But those who didn't see conspiracy in their movement weren't looking very hard. When I later flicked through my photo roll, I saw a great many homemade signs like the one carried by the woman in the dress – but the biggest banner by far was professionally printed and so large that a whole team of people was needed to hoist it into the air above the crowd.

It said, in foot-high black-and-white, letters: "COVID IS A HOAX."

In early 2021, as vaccines were gradually distributed in many countries and the world opened up for good, it was clear that anti-lockdown conspiracists would shift to anti-vaccine themes, and when reports of harm and a small number of deaths from vaccines began to appear in the media, it was similarly obvious that activists would start blaming all sorts of unrelated deaths on the shots. Conspiracy narratives are endlessly adaptable; if there had been delays in the research or rollout, it's quite possible that a narrative would have developed that elites had really found lifesaving treatments, but were keeping them away from ordinary people.

The anti-vax sentiment I saw on the streets of London had gained steam in the UK and elsewhere, and could even be traced back to Andrew Wakefield,[9] but it was American activists who were really driving the trend.

Not only was the anti-vaccine lobby soon part of the mainstream of MAGA and the Republican Party, it's one of the best examples I can think of to demonstrate how American populism now drives the politics of the entire Western world, and much else beyond. The messages that American anti-vaxxers pumped out took hold even in European countries with vastly different approaches to health care and the role of private enterprise within it.

In Britain, broad vaccine mandates were opposed by people across the political spectrum on civil liberties and human rights grounds. In contrast to what has long been law in many places in the United States, British kids don't have to get vaccinated against anything before attending school, and there's no real political drive to implement a mandatory vaccine program. Added to that mix is the National Health Service and a network of local pharmacists who are broadly trusted to dish out advice to the British public.[10]

Despite this, throughout 2020 and 2021 – on anti-lockdown marches and particularly online – I consistently came across arguments about mandates and the influence of pharmaceutical companies that were lifted wholesale from American sources, right down to the American spelling of certain words.

With few allies in mainstream politics and no real foothold in power, the British anti-vaxxers remained confined to the fringes. Take the differing fortunes of two right-wing politicians. Andrew Bridgen was a member of the UK Conservative Party and a member of Parliament for more than a decade before he began spreading vaccine conspiracy theories, at one point comparing Covid vaccine injuries to the Holocaust. He was summarily booted out of his party and will almost certainly not be an MP after the next UK general election.

Not so in the United States. Marjorie Taylor Greene has repeatedly spread anti-vax messages among her grab bag of conspiracy theories, like one about Rothschild-linked space lasers causing wildfires – a direct precursor to those Hawaii "directed energy weapon" rumors. In contrast to Bridgen, Greene was promoted to a powerful position in the House of Representatives.

The anti-vax energy was now coming from Americans, and by and large Americans who supported the Republican Party and Donald Trump. And yet the former president himself did not neatly fit into the anti-vax picture.

Although he had once spread groundless rumors about vaccines and autism,[11] Covid turned him into a vaccine enthusiast, and he launched Operation Warp Speed, the government program to super-charge vaccine development, in hopes of quelling the pandemic.[12] He received a shot himself – though not in public – and backed Covid vaccines even after leaving office.

"I believe totally in your freedoms. I do. You've got to do what you have to do," he told one rally. "But I recommend take the vaccines. I did it. It's good. Take the vaccines."

The crowds made their opinions about the shots known – at events in Alabama and Texas, Trump was actually booed.[13]

There were deeper values-based connections between the anti-vaxxers and the former president. They believe experts are wrong, the deep state is lying, elites are trying to control your life, and vested interests are corrupted by money and must be stopped at all costs. By 2023, anti-vaccine sentiment had taken over, and Trump was busy trying to paint his main rival as a vaccine enthusiast – which, among many MAGA Republicans, was considered a bad thing.[14]

"As a Republican, it's not a great thing to talk about," he said on Fox News that summer. "Because people love the vaccines and people hate the vaccines."[15]

Trump had found that he could not control the angry energy of the anti-vaxxers. Stew Peters, on the other hand, had built a mini-media empire off of all the fury.

"This is how you treat the FAKE MSM," he posted after our interview, pointing to a link of his own video of our encounter in a tweet that he left pinned to the top of his profile for months. Then, in an odd allegation about something broadcast around the world, he wrote: "BBC doesn't want you to see this."[16]

Of course, there would be no mass beheadings of medical experts, no jailing of journalists who had debunked Covid disinformation. Stew Peters and his fans were impotently howling into the void. In his mind, though, we were the delusional ones, thinking that we could debunk his falsehoods without encountering a backfire effect.

"All you're doing is empowering the people who want the truth," he fumed to us during the interview. "These people want a real leader, which is probably why after President Trump is indicted, I should probably be the president."

Again, I struggled to keep a straight face.

"Are you joking?" I asked.

"Do I look like I'm joking?" he growled.

"You want to be president?"

"Somebody's got to lead this country."

The idea of President Stew Peters was as preposterous as it was frightening, but I worried more about the people who might take him seriously. When they realized there would be no "Nuremberg 2.0" trials, that journalists weren't going to be executed, and that gay sex would continue to be perfectly legal, where would their attention turn next? Where would all the pent-up rage go? What might they do? As I found out, some people who were prepared to do much more than tweet were already getting much more extreme.

7

No political solution

In the summer of 2023, a video of Proud Boys, shot in a Portland suburb, went viral. It showed a protest against a Pride Month event in Oregon City.[1]

That much was predictable, but what happened next was the interesting part. A small throng of masked young men showed up. Words were exchanged, and the argument became more heated. The Proud Boys called the other group "racist" and used an anti-gay slur. They demanded that the other group take their masks off, and when they fail to comply, they ripped them off themselves. A brawl broke out. Two people were arrested.[2]

It seemed like a throwback to the regular political violence that I had reported on in Portland during the Trump years. But the masked men were not part of an anti-fascist cell — quite the opposite. They were fighting the Proud Boys from the right, and called themselves the Rose City Nationalists — a more extreme, explicitly white nationalist group. This was not a case of far-left and far-right activists duking it out, but rather a battle within the far-right fringes.

In right-wing circles online, the incident blew up. Sure enough, "psyop" and "false flag" claims popped up immediately. Amateur investigators claimed the Rose City Nationalists were not white nationalists at all, but antifa members or federal agents.

The evidence was flimsy and relied on at least one case of mistaken identity, but to the believers that didn't really matter.

Gavin McInnes, the Proud Boy founder, wrote on Telegram: "Masked Feds show up to Proud Boys event. PBs immediately call them out, tune them up, and demask them."[3] He went on: "I'm told this is one of the Patriot Front Feds the Proud Boys unmasked. He is Jewish and says he plans to work for the gov't after he graduates. Huge if true."[4]

It wasn't true. The man who was mistakenly identified, Ben Brody, was about a thousand miles away in southern California at the time of the fight and had nothing to do with either group save a slight physical resemblance to a member of the unmasked mob.

But the rumors went viral. Elon Musk posted: "Looks like one is a college student (who wants to join the govt) and another is maybe an Antifa member, but nonetheless a probable false flag situation," and tagged Community Notes, the site's crowdsourced fact-checking operation.[5] Several people pointed out Musk's error, but the tweet remained up. Brody later sued Musk for defamation.[6]

It was further evidence of just how deeply paranoia had set in; via the accounts of Musk and other influencers, millions were now engrossed in wild conspiracy theories about a supposedly manufactured tiff on the far right. Proud Boys plausibly believed that they were being targeted by the FBI, however for some reason they thought this targeting came not in the form of infiltrators or undercover agents, but a "fake" group which set out to create a manufactured fight. Following their convoluted stream of consciousness, this incident was somehow intended to discredit the Proud Boys in the eyes of the public, as if the group – whose leaders were about to face decades in jail for subversion against the government – had a sterling reputation to protect. It was fantasy-land stuff, but far-right leaders and those they held sway over pushed it hard anyway.

Away from the conspiratorial noise, the real story of the Oregon City brawl was developing online. Proud Boys Telegram channels were blowing up with debates over whether it was right to fight the white nationalist group or not. Splinter groups called "Active Clubs" cropped up – named after their focus on weightlifting and physical fitness – prompting more established Proud Boys chapters to respond with threats of violence.[7] One member angrily accused others of "betraying" Portland-area Proud Boys, being sure to make it clear that they were still totally against what they called "pedo drag hour."

It was a familiar pattern for those who had studied the alt-right, or other fringe movements – groups accused by their more hardcore members of failing to be radical enough fractured over time. That made them weaker, but it also had the potential to spawn more extreme, unpredictable elements. And after the dissolution of the alt-right and the mess of the Capitol riot, that's exactly what was happening.

January 6, 2021 created problems for far-right groups on three separate fronts. They were shut down by social media companies and lost much of their ability to organize and communicate online. Law enforcement crackdowns put leaders like Enrique Tarrio and Stewart Rhodes in jail and prompted ordinary members to start zapping accounts and deleting messages, hampering both communications and recruitment efforts. And as public pressure ramped up, so did the internal turf battles, pushed along by waves of paranoia, given additional fuel by revelations that fellow travelers were turning into informants or testifying against their former comrades.

The Proud Boys managed to survive, as I've noted, by changing focus towards anti-LGBTQ activity. Their chapter-based structure and emphasis on personal, in-real-life, beer-drinking connection helped the group weather the tough times of 2021. Gavin McInnes contended that the group he founded is "set in stone."

"There's no top, there's no head," he told me. "It's like the Hells Angels. Could you end the Hells Angels?"

The Three Percenters Militia – a group which took its name from the questionable belief that only a small proportion of American colonists actively resisted the British Army – is an even more decentralized anti-government organization, one based on local chapters sharing similar ideas, but no real overarching structure.[8] It too has persisted, but more in the guise of an overall idea and logo – based on the Roman numeral "III" – than a cohesive group. A number of Three Percenters were arrested for participation in the Capitol Riot, and six weeks after the mayhem, the national group that laid claim to the movement issued one last statement condemning the violence and bringing their organization to an end.[9] Local and state chapters, however, continue to operate.

The Oath Keepers have also not fared well. They were founded and driven from the start by Rhodes, and his son and ex-wife described to me and my colleagues the iron grip he maintained on the group – as well as nearly every aspect of their family life.[10] When he was arrested along with several of the group's other leaders, and a membership list was leaked, the Oath Keepers were decapitated and declawed, and no longer have much of a presence anywhere in the country.

Meanwhile, other far-right groups, lured by the possibility of clout, power and new recruits, have stepped into the power vacuum.

The pictures from Idaho were bizarre and frightening. Thirty-one young men, dressed similarly in khaki trousers and wearing masks over their faces, were hauled out of the back of a truck by police, who zip-tied their hands behind their backs and made them kneel by the side of a road.[11]

It was June 2022, and the gang was headed towards a Pride parade in Coeur d'Alene – a town that is both a genteel tourist hub and a focal point for the regional white nationalist movement in the Pacific Northwest. In the van, police found riot gear, a smoke grenade and shields. The men wore patches identifying them as members of a relatively new group: Patriot Front.[12]

Patriot Front was formed after Charlottesville as a splinter of Vanguard America, a neo-Nazi group that had itself been hamstrung by infighting and external pressure. Members mostly conceal their identities and post propaganda under the cover of darkness. On their website – its name taken directly from a Nazi slogan[13] – they post videos and maps of their activities.

Their explicitly white nationalist outlook incorporates a number of other far-right themes, and they're anti-Semitic, anti-LGBTQ, anti-government and anti-Native American – one of their propaganda posters reads "Stolen not conquered" over an outline of the United States. They are in fact obsessed with the theme of conquest and raw power struggles.

"Our national way of life faces complete annihilation as our culture and heritage are attacked from all sides," the Patriot Front manifesto reads.[14] "Americans are on the threshold of becoming a conquered people … A new tyranny must be met with a new resistance."

Patriot Front attracted a different cohort than the more established far-right groups. Unlike the Proud Boys – judging from news reports and arrest records – they tend to be younger, more covert and less focused on drinking beer. While not averse to an overt show of force like the operation in Idaho, most of their propaganda activity, which includes postering and stenciling, is carried out undercover, with a particular eye towards both concealing identities and maximizing recruitment value.

In 2021, leaked chats indicated the group had slightly more than 200 members.[15] But their impact has been far greater than that number would indicate. In 2022, the Anti-Defamation League (ADL) recorded a huge jump in white nationalist propaganda, the biggest wave that the organization had ever seen.[16] Patriot Front was responsible for the vast majority of these incidents – around 80 percent. Their banners, stickers and posters went up in every state except for Hawaii and Alaska.

They reveled in ambiguity and dabbled in diversifying their message. In addition to the racist slogans, some of their banners read "No more foreign wars" and "Defend American labor" – catchphrases that wouldn't look out of place in a mainstream political campaign. Another stenciled sign read "Reject poison," with icons of a needle, a marijuana leaf, pills and a cigarette. These were definitely not the hard-partying Proud Boys.

The ADL reported that two other fringe groups are responsible for a significant chunk of white nationalist propaganda. The Goyim Defense League (GDL), its name taken from the Hebrew word for non-Jews, distributed blunt flyers aiming to "expose" Jewish control of society. The GDL was particularly active in Florida, where a number of anti-Semitic incidents prompted a rare expansion of hate crimes laws by a Republican governor in April 2023.[17]

The third group is White Lives Matter, which distributes similarly artless screeds about the "great replacement" conspiracy theory – the idea that there is a secret (usually described as "Jewish-controlled") plot to end the white race through a combination of lower birth rates, immigration, and interracial relationships.

Together, the three groups were responsible, the ADL said, for 93 percent of the white nationalist incidents it had recorded – more than 6,700 nationwide.

These groups and others like them — including organizations such as The Base and the Nationalist Front — currently make up the more extreme organized far-right. They're explicit in their beliefs, but unfriendly towards the media.

They have a curious relationship to the rest of the right-wing fringes. Sometimes, there are real ideological differences, but just as often they are the target of conspiracy theories, paranoia, and a desire to avoid bad publicity. They are like embarrassing, unstylish cousins who always say the wrong thing. In their masks and khaki trousers, Patriot Front makes the right-wing fringes look like a bunch of threatening office workers, rather than alt-right trendies or proud, hard-working Americans. But instead of distancing themselves from such groups, others on the right-wing activist fringes insist they are antifa plants, government "psyop" agents or undercover feds.

In May 2023, Patriot Front members briefly emerged once again from the cover of darkness. More than 100 supporters marched through Washington, holding makeshift shields, flags and bullhorns.[18] They weren't well received by locals and tourists, including a cyclist who became momentarily famous for mocking the masked marchers with bon mots like "You look like General Custer's illegitimate son."[19]

Sure enough, on Twitter, on Reddit and in other far-right and conservative forums, groundless accusations flew about federal agents and nefarious government plots. The supposed aim of the "plot" was rarely if ever articulated (To radicalize young people? Bolster support for hate crime laws? Make neo-Nazis look foolish?). But in some quarters it quickly became the dominant narrative.

"No Patriot group I've ever seen wears khakis, Stormtrooper knee pads, and covers their faces like they're scared," tweeted Marjorie Taylor Greene. "Just more movie characters."

"They are a false flag FBI (or other federal agents) pretending?" asked another popular Twitter account. "Or a real group of protesters?"[20]

You can guess which side most of the thousands of replies landed on. There was, of course, no evidence that the Patriot Front members had ties to law enforcement, federal or otherwise, although by now, given what we know about radical groups, it's a strong possibility that agents have infiltrated their ranks. In addition to their clothing – which was described as either too neat or too close to what FBI agents wear (curiously, those same khakis also happen to be the typical casual work uniform of the American male), paranoiacs also asked why the police didn't halt the march. It was another odd thing to query – a cohort so obsessed with free speech had momentarily forgotten about the First Amendment.

Patriot Front and similar groups would consistently be dogged by these accusations, which flared up any time they tried to rally in public. Whether the rumors had an effect on operations or recruiting is difficult to say.

But hidden even further underground were smaller, more radical right-wing groups which completely shunned public protests. Among them were accelerationists hell bent on destruction. Their numbers are even smaller, but they were starting to package their ideas as a semi-cohesive whole. And they were trying to take the end times paranoia of the American far right to its ultimate and logical conclusion.

In July 2022, the latest of a series of do-it-yourself terrorism instruction booklets appeared online.

It was called *The Hard Reset*. The title was a play on The Great Reset, an initiative invented by the World Economic Forum that became better known for inspiring a number of conspiracy theories about world government, enslavement of whole populations and forced vaccinations.

The Hard Reset and its companion titles weren't viral hits. They couldn't be easily found, even on message boards like 4chan and 8kun. Nor were they particularly steeped in the levity of online culture. I was advised by several terrorism researchers not to actively seek them out, so of course I immediately started searching. Before too long, I was reading a set of sabotage and propaganda manuals that was both deadly serious and, potentially, just plain deadly. The booklets were produced by a loose anonymous confederation dubbed "Terrorgram" and are a window into the thinking of some of the most extreme fascists in America today.

The image of a white-hooded, cross-burning, knuckle-dragging KKK redneck persists in the popular imagination. But these manuals showed a different level of sophistication and forethought, along with a strong aesthetic sensibility. They resembled punk zines or DIY concert posters. The format was bold, simple, in-your-face – even before considering the content.

They were instruction manuals and propaganda sheaves, full of lurid fictional fantasies about war and glorification of mass murder. They included screeds against modern technology – an interesting touch, given their electronic means of distribution – and environmental and pro-wilderness eco-fascist themes. They provided instructions for stockpiling weapons and supplies and encouraged acts of terror in order to destabilize society and bring about a white nationalist revolution – a hallmark of the fascist branch of accelerationism. This is the lethal edge of the most extreme far-right, people who believe they can realize their goals by speeding up the rate of social change – precipitating a racial holy war through terror and violence. In one of the few "lighter" touches, recipes for explosives were written in a language millions of young people understand: Minecraft icons.

There were a few other interesting details in the terror manuals. They claimed to be written by dozens of collaborators writing under pseudonymous tags such as "National Accelerationist Revival," "Pobox" and "Right Wing Book Club," or just letters of the alphabet. I had my doubts about whether all of these writers were separate individuals, as some of their writing styles seemed very similar. But there was no denying that the series was the work of a small group of people, involving a certain level of co-ordination and operational security. Terrorists are sometimes called "lone wolves," but far from isolated individuals, attackers often have an anonymous pack behind them, egging them on, feeding them ideas and glorifying violent acts until more bloodshed becomes inevitable. In Terrorgram's writings, I had stumbled upon the wolf pack.

Interspersed between explosives formulas and race hate, there were strangely personal stories and parables about how young men should live – self-sufficiently, in small towns, well-armed, surviving on a diet consisting mostly of raw meat. One odd anecdote related in way-too-graphic detail the story of a bout of food poisoning that the author had been afflicted with after munching on uncooked supermarket liver. The takeaway was: don't rely on supply chains, big companies, capitalism or the trappings of urban life – you will end up sick.

The militant far-right glorifies mass murderers as "saints," a technique with a long history intended to draw others into the radical fold.[21] *The Hard Reset* even hinted that one of Terrorgram's next publications would be a "Saint Encyclopedia." The idea of worshipping murderers has its roots in Nazi propaganda, and was revived in the American white nationalist and militia movements of the 20th century.

A decade ago, incel groups began to venerate a 22-year-old Californian who, motivated by hatred of women and disappointment at sexual rejection, killed six people and injured 14 others. The California attacker was directly referenced years later by a man who drove into a Toronto crowd, killing 11 people: "All hail the Supreme Gentleman," he wrote on Facebook. The Christchurch attacker has similarly been held aloft as a virtuous "saint" by the Buffalo attacker and others.

This peculiar idea of sainthood and the prospect of glory held out to young men living otherwise unremarkable lives in forgotten towns has helped to perpetuate a cycle of far-right violence.

The offshoots of this hardcore political philosophy crop up in unusual ways. Accelerationists linked with the strange but deadly boogaloo movement had a brief moment of attention in 2020 after members killed two law enforcement officials and were involved in other attempted attacks. The so-called Boogaloo Bois saw opportunity to foment their vision of civil war in the unrest surrounding protests over George Floyd's murder and the 2020 election.

But as accelerationist ideas have gathered momentum – and as repeated mass slaughters have not resulted in the race war that the militants crave – some have set their destructive sights on a different target: aiming to take down the power grid.

In March 2023, two people were arrested and charged with trying to knock out power to the city of Baltimore.

Brandon Russell and Sarah Clendaniel began talking while both were in prison. Russell is the founder of Atomwaffen Division, a violent neo-Nazi organization that has been linked to a long list of murders and violent attacks. Clendaniel, who robbed stores and was a drug addict, was pictured wearing a skull mask and brandishing a gun.[22] They were plotting more than the violent murders of a dozen or two dozen people. Clendaniel said she hoped that their attack "would completely destroy the whole city."

An investigation by the Program on Extremism at George Washington University concluded that since 2016, white supremacist plots targeting energy systems have dramatically increased in frequency.[23] The experts found 11 cases of white nationalists arrested and charged in federal court with planning attacks on the energy sector since 2020.

"The chance that someone is able to pull off an attack of this nature is substantial," said Bennett Clifford, a senior research fellow at the program.

In other words, according to Veryan Khan, head of the Terrorism Research & Analysis Consortium, "it's not a matter of if, it's when." She told me that she'd seen more and more online chatter, particularly on Telegram, encouraging far-right radicals to carry out attacks against infrastructure.

"In terms of noise level, the pounding of the drum is almost deafening," she said in early 2023.

Accelerationists are more interested in causing chaos than in claiming responsibility. Individual terrorists – for instance, a murderer who killed two men outside a gay bar in Slovakia[24] – have declared their support for Terrorgram or allied movements, but the groups themselves do not make claims around attacks in the same way that, for instance, al Qaeda does. That strategy has kept people guessing about several recent assaults.

In North Carolina in December 2022, more than 40,000 people were left without power when someone fired at two electricity substations. Court documents indicate Brandon Russell and Sarah Clendaniel were aware of the attack and perhaps inspired by it. They viewed YouTube videos about it, possibly to glean technical tips. At the time of writing, nobody's been arrested for the North Carolina attack, and the motive behind it remains unclear.

But the radicals of Terrorgram will have certainly noted that the attack, and other similar assaults, have not yet caused mass panic or civil war. They'll be looking out for ways to further up the ante, increase the chaos and spread the damage.

And while their tactics may be different, viewed in one way the far-right accelerationist idea of a cleansing racial holy war is a more extreme version of the ambitions of another movement, whose leaders talk openly about injecting religious values into the heart of government.

Unlike the accelerationists or the neo-Nazis of Patriot Front, Christian nationalists do not lurk in the shadows. They're building a broad popular nationwide movement. They couch their advocacy in typical American tropes about God and family. They eschew violence, or at least, nihilistic violence. They appeal to many people beyond the fringes. And, largely away from the glare of the media, they've captured the support of very powerful people.

8

Christian nationalists
and radical moms

A few miles inland from the city of Venice on Florida's south-west Gulf coast there's a place called The Hollow 2A. It's a sprawling 10-acre compound that includes a campground, a wedding venue, picnic areas, a butterfly pavilion, a small underground museum dedicated to America's founding fathers, and a gun range.[1]

The Hollow hosts a variety of seasonal events. Online videos and advertisements show off light shows, 4th of July fireworks displays and a Christmas celebration complete with fake snow.

"The family aspect is the norm," says owner Vic Mellor. "The political events are an anomaly. We don't have them that often but that's what we get attention for."

There may be a reason for that.

The Hollow's website describes it as a "freedom loving, American values sanctuary" that "works as a uniting force to assist in connecting freedom loving Patriot groups." On its website there is a mission statement: "How does a handful of people (535) in Washington abuse and manipulate 350 million people ... We allowed it.

"The Hollow 2A is the place where Americans gather to lawfully take back our country," the statement continues. "Consistent with the United States Constitution and the Florida Constitution, the Hollow 2A is mandate free, mask free and censor-free." On the top of the page there is a photo of a man supervising a child, who is aiming a gun. Mellor, who was present outside the Capitol during the January 6 riot, also owns a number of other businesses in the Venice area, including a "vaccine-free" health clinic.

Since it opened in 2019, The Hollow has attracted crowds of ordinary people, but also Republican operatives, a Proud Boys-affiliated pressure group, members of local conservative groups and churches. It's where anti-vaccine, pro-gun, pro-Trump families gather among like-minded people to drink in a certain type of American history, and often a strong dose of religion – although Mellor told me he's no Christian.

"I don't need God to identify evil," he told me. "I can see evil on my own. There's a lot of people like me that aren't religious, that are part of The Hollow, and part of this nationalist movement."

In divided but increasingly conservative Florida, The Hollow has become an ideal launch pad for revived spirit of nationalist fervor that has solidified an alliance among supporters of evangelical conservativism, the patriot movement, QAnon and Donald Trump.

The United States is, of course, a country where a large majority of people consider themselves religious. Most are Christian, and God is frequently invoked in public life.[2]

But most Americans also believe in the separation of church and state along the lines laid out in the US Constitution. Prayer is not required in public schools; there's no religious oath required to take public office. This has created a peculiar kind of tension in American society, where faith and secularism are in a constant sort of tug-of-war. Throughout American history, dating back to colonial times, great waves of religious fervor have regularly burst out in a series of "Great Awakenings," spilling out of churches into cultural and political life.

The same phrase has very deliberately been used by QAnon adherents to describe their own movement, and by conspiracy theorist Alex Jones as the title of one of his books.

Christian nationalists want to chip away at church–state divisions or destroy them entirely. Although it's a rather nebulous concept which means vastly different things to different Americans,[3] the strain that has come to the fore in recent years wraps together not just worship of Jesus, gun rights and opposition to abortion, but anti-vaccine and election conspiracies and support for Donald Trump. Its proponents argue that Christians should actively seek to make the United States into a nation led by Christians and bake religious concepts into law.

As with the anti-vaccination movement, Trump would seem to be a less-than-ideal standard bearer for Christian nationalism – a man who keeps any humility or piety he may have well hidden. But Trump and his advisors understand that evangelical Christians are dedicated Republican voters, and have capitalized on issues like abortion. Trump-appointed Supreme Court justices were key in overturning *Roe v Wade*. On his Truth Social account, the former president has shared images comparing himself to Jesus, and his series of arrests supercharged such comparisons, with his supporters calling him a "martyr." It helped that Trump's arrest in New York came shortly before Easter.

"Seems there was someone else who was tortured and crucified this week," one user wrote on Gab, a social network populated mostly by the far-right.[4]

Among some of his fans, Trump's image has become so messianic and infused with the end-times urgency of the 2024 campaign that it's more accurate to call this wave MAGA Christian Nationalism.

Many actually do believe Trump is acting on direct orders from God. His campaign leans into themes of persecution, redemption and salvation. To take just one example, a fundraising email from October 2023 had the simple subject line "Faith." It read: "The Left wants to crush our hope and break our spirit. They want to rob us of our joy ... Your faith is the one thing no one can ever take from you." It concluded: "So, my question to you is: do YOU have faith that America can be saved? If you do, please make a contribution of even $1 to SAVE AMERICA in 2024."

From a candidate, particularly on the right of American politics, this is arguably not out of the ordinary. But the former president's supporters repeat the supposedly divine message and translate it into their own language. In one of the massive Facebook groups dedicated to his fandom, I came across dozens and dozens of messages typifying this attitude, such as: "President Trump stands for we the people and the Lord, if we don't have the Lord God, President Trump wouldn't be doing the things he's doing, he's the best president we've ever had." Some observers were left dumbfounded shortly before the 2024 Iowa caucus, when the former president shared a fan-made video on Truth Social with the title "God Made Trump."

One of its most influential proponents of MAGA Christian Nationalism is Michael Flynn, who in early 2017 held the post of national security advisor in the Trump administration for a total of 22 days. Flynn got in trouble for mischaracterizing his conversations with Russia's ambassador to the United States, and later pleaded guilty to lying the FBI. Most three-week appointees who face criminal charges gradually fade away to punchlines and golf courses, but Flynn stuck around in Trump's orbit – the president granted him a pardon – and was still informally advising Trump around the time of the 2020 election and beyond.

A career army man who was the chief of military intelligence under Barack Obama, over time Flynn – a proud Christian – gradually got sucked into conspiracy world. He took an oath to QAnon and headlined ReAwaken America, a travelling Christian nationalist roadshow where he urged supporters to join him in a political and spiritual war.[5] One investigative report called the tour "a petri dish for Christian nationalism" which "pushes the idea that there's a battle underway between good and evil forces."[6] Biblical concepts are a constant theme in Flynn's public appearances. At one ReAwaken stop, in November 2021, Flynn declared: "If we are going to have one nation under God, which we must, we have to have one religion. One nation under God, and one religion under God."[7]

Flynn[8] lives in the Sarasota area, is friends with Mellor, holds events at The Hollow and records his podcast at a studio there.[9] In September 2021, during a speech, he outlined his vision for the future,[10] in which America's representational democracy has withered away or been blown apart, to be replaced by a theocracy. He invoked a grand sweep of history and told the gathering that struggles to maintain American democracy presented an opportunity rather than a problem.

"The republic of the United States of America, we have to look at ourselves kind of like the moon waxing and waning," he said. "The pathway or the destiny of this country can be wherever we want it to be."

Black Lives Matter was a communist front, he contended, in league with the Democratic Socialists of America to impose dictatorship. The 2020 election was rigged, he went on, and all the proof anyone needed for these statements was the fact that a great many people wore red MAGA hats, but nobody wore clothing promoting President Biden or his "Build Back Better" legislative plan. The audience did not need persuading, for they knew they knew the truth.

"The opposition we are facing, they are masters of distraction, they are masters of programming," he said. "This is an unprecedented time in America. We have never been here before ... This is a very very spiritual war we are involved in."

Flynn's visions fit into a long tradition of apocalyptic thinking, projected onto the current political moment and amping up the paranoia of the right. The Hollow 2A crowd erupted in applause.

MAGA Christian Nationalism has set down roots in evangelical churches and other religious spaces that have long been aligned with Republican and conservative values. But there are fresh new avenues where the themes of the movement have resonated, particularly among women. Flynn's speech was part of a conference organized by a group called Moms for America. The group uses a Thomas Jefferson quote as their motto: "Adore God. Reverence and cherish your parents. Love your neighbor as yourself and country more than yourself." Its website is peppered with references to God-given rights fused with the American style of liberty.

The group also bought fully and completely into election conspiracy theories. Moms for America organized pro-Trump rallies in Washington on January 5 and 6, 2021. At one, newly sworn-in Congresswoman Mary Miller, a member of the Freedom Caucus, said: "Hitler was right on one thing. He said, 'Whoever has the youth has the future.' Our children are being propagandized." After the Capitol riot, she apologized.[11]

The Moms for America year-end report later boasted of more than 500 media appearances, including on Fox, One America News, Breitbart and Newsmax. It might not be a household name outside of a right-wing bubble, but it has steadily grown in influence and connections. Founder Kimberly Fletcher spoke at a ReAwaken America event, and the group said its members had won school board seats in 17 different states.[12] The group mirrored high-profile student strikes with its own "parents strike" against mask mandates, vaccine mandates and what it called "institutionalized child abuse."

Any confusion between Moms for America and a similar-sounding group, Moms for Liberty, is entirely understandable; the two groups have similar goals and platforms. Moms for America, which was originally known as Home-Makers for America, has been around for two decades. But it was the younger association, Moms for Liberty, which truly injected right-wing ideas into maternal politics and grabbed the spotlight during the pandemic and beyond.

Moms for Liberty was founded in 2021 by three south Florida mothers. Initially, the women were spurred to action by their opposition to mask and vaccine mandates, but their platform expanded into other areas, particularly opposition to what they called "woke indoctrination" of children, and support for removing books that discuss gender and race from schools. Moms for Liberty has dropped most of the explicitly religious language while keeping the focus on culture war issues and the idea of an end-times battle. Its website declares the group is "dedicated to fighting for the survival of America" – not just devoted to children or the family – and in a podcast and promotional material, the moms describe themselves as "joyful warriors." Perhaps as a result, the group has appealed to an even wider cross-section of the public.

"We don't co-parent with the government" is one of their key slogans, and in practice this means they insist on near-total parental control of the public school educational curriculum and learning materials, along with an end to public health mandates in schools. Most of the time they make news via local campaigns to remove books with themes they would rather their children not be exposed to – invariably these involve gender, sexuality, race and so on – from public school libraries. But their main means by which to achieve their ends is to get members and other candidates they endorse elected to local school boards.

By a number of measures, Moms for Liberty has been incredibly successful. In two years, the organization says it has established nearly 300 chapters with 120,000 active members. Its Florida roots and opposition to "wokeness" cast its members as allies of Ron DeSantis, but Trump and other high-profile Republicans spoke at its 2023 national conference, which was quickly becoming a required destination for conservative politicians.

The group may have played off of traditional stereotypes of motherhood and childhood innocence, but not all members were exactly quiet cookie-baking types. One chapter chair in Pennsylvania was arrested on a charge of harassment; another member in Arkansas mused about shooting a local librarian, and a QAnon-believing chapter leader in Michigan was hit with a restraining order.[13] A Florida member suggested that gay and straight students be taught in separate classrooms.[14]

And like the other maternal group, Moms for Liberty could somehow not avoid Hitler controversy. A chapter newsletter in Indiana used the same quote that Congresswoman Miller had cited, slightly tweaked: "He alone who OWNS the youth, GAINS the future." The chapter apologized, but several days later, at the same annual conference that drew so many Republican luminaries, the group's top organizers took a different tack.[15]

"There's always a reason something happens, right?" said co-founder Tiffany Justice.

"One of our moms in a newsletter quotes Hitler," she continued. One or two audience members whooped. Then Justice delivered the kicker: "I stand with that mom."

Although an uncharitable interpretation could be that Justice was endorsing Hitler, it's more accurate to say that she was embracing the Trumpian style of public relations: never apologize, never back down, never admit you're wrong.

The assembled moms loved it. The crowd went wild.[16]

Back in southwest Florida, one story that emerged in the summer of 2022 showed just how successful Moms for Liberty and the broader "parental rights" movement had become, and how the far-right web had come to connect various groups who put aside any differences they might have had to advance their collective goals.

A slate of conservative candidates ran for Sarasota County's school board, among them the incumbent Bridget Ziegler, another Moms for Liberty co-founder.[17] Sarasota County itself is a mix of coastal cities, suburbs and large rural areas. Politically, it sways in the tropical breeze; voters went for Obama twice, then Trump twice.

The conservative candidates ran an aggressive woke-bashing and culture war campaign. At one point, someone drove around a mobile billboard calling an opposition candidate "BABY KILLER."[18] They had a wide network of supporters: Ron DeSantis, Steve Bannon, Flynn, the owners and patrons of The Hollow, and nearby Proud Boys.[19] It worked. The conservatives won. And they kept on adding to their local power across the country. By the end of 2023, Moms for Liberty claimed in a press release to have won a total of 365 school board seats. Outside observers noticed they had lost most races, including in some of the areas where their contentious ideas had received the most attention.[20] But there was no doubt that the group was picking up members and gradually gaining power in local politics in friendly places around the country.

Even in areas that are more politically mixed, a combination of factors has enabled Moms for Liberty and its allies to gain power. On Florida's Gulf Coast, the right-wing ecosystem seemed to be thriving in advance of 2024. The video-sharing site Rumble, a favorite among far-right activists, is headquartered nearby, as is Trump's Truth Social.[21] And riding the MAGA Christian Nationalist wave, Flynn has gone from outcast to hero. In June 2023, the ReAwaken America tour held an event at a Trump resort in Miami. Speakers included

Eric Trump, Truth Social CEO Devin Nunes and former Trump administration officials.

When Flynn took the stage, the crowd was already buzzing. Then Trump himself phoned in, heaping praise on the former general.

"You just have to stay healthy because we're bringing you back," the former president said. "I want to thank General Flynn for being a very brave man who was absolutely tortured. He's stronger now than he ever was, and it takes someone very special to pull that off."[22] After he won the 2024 election, Trump said, he'd welcome the general back into the White House.

MAGA Christian Nationalists hoped to ride a reborn Trump campaign to power through their chosen one, and the south Florida network had an audience of millions through its organizations and tech companies. But the circle of influencers pushing fringe ideas was much wider than people like Flynn and his cohorts.

Although many had taken a hit from the Capitol riot and Trump's departure from office, the new influencers of the far-right certainly didn't go away. They comprise a sort of shadow system, utilizing online platforms to great effect and working across media, becoming more powerful than traditional outlets when it comes to shaping the views of large sections of the American right. These influencers feed off of perpetual grievance of being shut out of the mainstream – even as they continue tunneling underground, even further towards centers of power.

9

The perpetual influencer machine

In late August 2023, a hurricane was bearing down on the west coast of Florida. I went to Tampa, a few hours north of Sarasota, to cover the story. In the day before it hit, I drove from shelter to shelter, talking to residents who had come to wait out the storm.

The weather started sunny and muggy, but waves of rain soon swept in. Outside a Wal-Mart, people were loading up cars with food and bottled water. As I made my way around the city, I tuned into a local talk radio show.

"Stocking up is good advice," said the host, adding: "But if I were you, I'd start buying masks and hand sanitizer instead, you're going to need it for the Covid lockdowns that are coming down the pipe later this year."

"You know, that's what I'm hearing on these conspiracy websites," he continued. "It's funny, these websites, they call them conspiracy sites, but they somehow always turn out to be right a few months ahead of time."

In the United States today, you can hear similar sentiments all the time, not just on conservative talk radio stations, but in local newspapers, on Facebook groups, in backyard cookouts and dive bars all across the country. It was a popular illusion, and easy to achieve: pump out a firehose of predictions and speculative statements, celebrate the ones that come true, never again mention the ones that don't.[1]

The strategy is so effective that it is routinely used by a huge cohort of podcasters and social media talking heads chasing money and clout. Although they don't disguise their political beliefs and rarely take part in the type of activities that used to be considered the core of journalism – traveling to places, asking questions to people directly involved in news events, grilling public leaders, weighing up and accurately reflecting arguments on various sides – these new influencers have capitalized on division and the fracturing effects of social media to gain big audiences. For millions of people, they have become a major source of information – supplanting the so-called "mainstream media" and even the right-wing talk show hosts like the ones I listened to in Tampa, the ones who in past decades formed the vanguard of the rightward push of American politics.

These new influencers are now the power brokers and the ideas merchants (and the T-shirt and vitamin supplement merchants) for a huge chunk of Republican America. Who are they – and what are they pushing?

"The fact is, Alex believes in everything he says," she said. "One-hundred and ten percent."

A light rain tapped on the roof as I talked to Kelly Jones, the ex-wife of the conspiratorial media mogul Alex Jones. It was December 2018, and we were sitting in a small, converted greenhouse outside their former family home, on the outskirts of Austin, Texas. Somewhere beneath us was enough dried food and ready-to-eat meals to feed a family for several years – evidence, Kelly told me, that Alex wasn't faking his belief in the impending apocalypse.

Here, above ground, Alex Jones' house was normal, or maybe hypernormal. The yard was littered with huge plaster casts of circus animals, surrounding a lush pool – a playground for the couple's children. The property was surrounded by a tall wall with a heavy, remote-control gate. The grounds were dotted with the hearty, multi-hued vegetation of central Texas.

Alex Jones had made a lot of money selling survivalist gear and vitamin supplements – enough to spend $100,000 a month even while in the midst of bankruptcy proceedings[2] – and his home reflected his vast wealth. His ex-wife, like the estranged wife of Stewart Rhodes, had early on been incredibly involved in the family business, and later on thoroughly disgusted with the whole thing.

"The thing that was really just shocking to me was how he built his foundation, his core following, off of very family-oriented people in the American Midwest," Kelly Jones told me. "It was a family show, and he was suddenly just so vulgar and crass and, and obscene."

Alex Jones had been broadcasting for decades but had increasingly filled his rants with fantasies about gang rapes of politicians and Hollywood actresses, genital mutilation, and descriptions of sickening and grotesque violence, especially against children. At times it was difficult to tell whether he was warning or fantasizing. It was the culmination of a long march from government-skeptic libertarianism and even anarchy – Alex Jones had, after all, once appealed to a significant slice of the anti-war left after the attacks of September 11, 2001 – to paranoid, reactionary politics. His audience-chasing was a good sign of where the fringes were going, and he'd become a sort of litmus test for a sprawling movement – were you willing to tolerate Jones, or were you a libtard who wanted him thrown out of the tent? Fans didn't believe everything he said, but many believed he'd been proven right about lots of things. Most of all – like Trump – he was saying things that were supposedly going "unsaid." Except that they were being said, repeatedly, every day and ad nauseam, in the alt-right online ecosystem.

I asked Kelly Jones: in the two decades since she had met her ex-husband, had he become more hardline in his views, or had his audience shifted, become angrier and fringier? Probably both, she said. They fed off of each other.

"With regards to conspiracy theories, we went from JFK [assassination theories] to Pizzagate," Kelly Jones told me. "Those are very different things, and that was really disturbing."

Amid all the talk of the New World Order, deep state, globalist plots and illuminati scheming, one obsession of Alex Jones' had come front and center, something he talked about all the time in the most blunt language – child sexual abuse. It was this focus, the way he used the issue as a cudgel, and his graphic descriptions, which bothered Kelly Jones the most.

"Talking in the way that he does about it, just throwing horrible words out that you would never even be able to say, like –" she stopped short. "I can't even say it. It's so disturbing to me."

Alex Jones was one of the OGs and at one point the undisputed king of an alternative universe, an entire nebulous infrastructure of podcasts, journalists, YouTubers, public intellectual types and others devoted to undermining a narrative they believed had become incontrovertible gospel in the United States and across the Western world.

In many ways, it's difficult to categorize this ecosystem and somewhat tricky to group all of their ideas and personalities together. They come with a web of internecine personality clashes, and the occasional ideological disagreement. Mentioning any of these people in the same breath as others will trigger howls of outrage – that the mainstream media machine is lying again, trying to lump them all together.

Not all of them are extremists, and not all of them promote violence. Many of them deny not only that they are on the far right, but that they are on the right of politics at all. But they do share a number of common points of view that, I think, enable us to broadly establish their general worldview, a worldview that is largely in line with current American far-right thought.

Generally, they are highly skeptical of Covid vaccines – some are not outwardly anti-vaccination, but most buy into stories about large numbers of Covid vaccine injuries are being hidden or downplayed at the behest of shadowy government or big business actors. They broadly agree that transgender activists and something called "wokeism" are overwhelming public institutions and private enterprise, and that Western governments and social media companies are engaged in comprehensive online censorship. They have given this fuzzy concept a catchy name: the Censorship Industrial Complex. They see hidden messages in world events, particularly in the conflict in Ukraine, and fervently believe they are being targeted by "cancel culture," however defined (their definitions are, by necessity, variable). A deep state is preserving a status quo, they say, that is murderously neo-conservative, communist or fascist (or sometimes, depending on which podcaster or presidential candidate you're listening to, all three at the same time).

Together they are oppositional – in fact, in contrast to the serious and powerful political actors they set themselves up against, they generally have few positive policy prescriptions and little long-term thinking. One description of them might be "anti-progressives"; it's easier to identify what they are against than what they are for. Those who broadly define themselves on the right rail against leftists, while others claim to come from a left-wing background yet feel they have been abandoned by their "own side." They believe that progressivism – in the realms of race, the environment, policing and economics – is an evil specter, both dominating the Western world and, at the same time, weakening US and other Western societies beyond recognition. And they're not just willing to entertain conspiracy theories – they revel in the transgression implied by the term. Like that talk show host in Tampa, they see the "conspiracy theory" label as something of a quality mark, a stamp that the "mainstream" or "liberal" media put on things they don't like. And so, by their logic, the conspiracy theorists must be right.

The people who comprise this anti-progressive bloc include Trump's most dedicated stalwarts – Steve Bannon, Roger Stone, Michael Flynn, plus key members of the House Freedom Caucus and officials in Republican states across the country. Even Trump opponents like Florida Governor Ron DeSantis broadly agree with this group, and many of them are DeSantis supporters, or were when his campaign looked as if it might take off as a viable alternative to Trump. Throughout 2023, the Trump–DeSantis tussle got progressively nastier and more personal, and the Florida governor appeared to get the worst of it, but he was not alone. All of the candidates for the Republican nomination who had a hope of winning were straining to capture the populist far-right rather than to carve out some new political terrain outside of Trump's orbit. It was, as many pundits said, Trump's Republican Party now.[3]

Viewed more broadly, the influencer ecosystem extended beyond Trump stalwarts. Anti-progressive ideas were regularly bellowed by the likes of Tucker Carlson, Joe Rogan and the British actor Russell Brand. Brand claimed to be broadly from the left, as did podcasters like Jimmy Dore and Tim Pool, and journalists like Glenn Greenwald and Matt Taibbi, though how to position them on a political spectrum these days was itself the subject of endless debate on other podcasts. Team anti-progressive even had an independent presidential candidate in Robert F. Kennedy Jr., a wealthy member of a political dynasty who had achieved sudden new relevance during the

Covid pandemic at the helm of America's anti-vaccination movement. Kennedy initially started running on his family legacy and consistently described himself as a "liberal," but when I floated around a crowd that had come to watch him in Michigan, just days before he dropped out of the Democratic Party primary, it was clear that his views on vaccination and the war in Ukraine were also drawing in a significant bloc of solidly conservative voters.[4]

Elon Musk's purchase of Twitter in 2022 gave this movement a natural home on a mainstream social network. As noted previously, Musk's tweets became more and more aligned with far-right and conspiratorial ideas – although it's tough to tell whether that was because the billionaire felt suddenly liberated to unleash long-held beliefs on the world or whether he had increasingly come under the sway of the environment he had become immersed in and now owned outright. A revealing biography stated that Musk's recent political transformation had been shaped by a transgender daughter who went to an elite private school and had cut off all contact with him.[5]

Whatever the reason, soon after buying X/Twitter, Musk moved to bring journalists into his orbit, including Bari Weiss, Taibbi and Michael Shellenberger – each of whom had diverse political backgrounds, but were signed up to the broader anti-progressive agenda. The X/Twitter boss let the group look at the so-called "Twitter Files" – internal emails and documents from the company's previous owners – and write complex threads which they said outlined the extent of government interference in social media.

X/Twitter was not alone in providing a haven for far-right influencers. There were a number of other sites that cropped up under the "alt-tech" banner. Rumble, the video-sharing site based in Florida, was a favorite for conspiratorial documentary makers and hosted *2000 Mules* and *Died Suddenly*. Far-right video makers could also choose from sites like

BitChute, DLive and Odysee. Gab.com, a sort of Twitter clone with a frog mascot, was run by a Christian nationalist in Pennsylvania. Despite its founders initially insisting that it would be home to a diverse collection of communities, it quickly devolved into an almost exclusively far-right space.[6] A man who killed 11 people at a Pittsburgh synagogue had an account on Gab. Just before carrying out his mass slaughter, he wrote: "Screw your optics, I'm going in." It was a reference to an ongoing discussion in white nationalist circles about whether far-right agitators should hide their hatred or be open about it.[7] Gab's CEO was called as a witness at the mass murderer's trial.[8]

Added to this alt-tech bunch were Donald Trump's Truth Social and Gettr, founded by Trump aide Jason Miller. Both were essentially echo chambers for Trump fans. Parler, a far-right network that was financially backed by the Mercer family,[9] played a key communications role during the Capitol riot. After the riot, it went offline for a while before pulling back from its fundamentalist anti-moderation stance. It closed down in 2023.[10]

Not only are there plenty of video sites and social networks, but an active system of podcasts, Telegram channels, blogs and other online avenues have provided launch pads for all sorts of anti-progressives, from intellectual types like Jordan Peterson, Michael Anton, Naomi Wolf and Curtis Yarvin – the blogger "Mencius Moldbug" – to attention hoarders like anti-Muslim congressional candidate Laura Loomer, to people who go by names like "Catturd," "Bronze Age Pervert," "LibsofTikTok" and "illuminatibot" on Musk's X/ Twitter.

And the ecosystem has plenty of room for former alt-right superstars, people like Mike Cernovich – a rape apologist who guest hosted for Alex Jones – and Jack Posobiec, a Pizzagate hype man who parlayed his social media influence into a role on the far-right One America News. One America and another far-right channel, Newsmax, became Fox News stalking horses on the far right, experiencing a spike in popularity after January 6, 2021, and freaking out Fox executives[11] to the point where they assisted in pushing election fraud rumors and got into legal trouble, which led to an enormous payout to voting machine company Dominion. Both One America and Newsmax pumped out highly partisan content more frequently seen on social media than on traditional cable television – and were much more popular online than they were on American televisions.

Those looking for news filtered through a right-wing lens had a huge array of choice beyond Fox News. There was Breitbart, of course, the one-time home of Steve Bannon[12] which, through several of its writers, became one of the key drivers of the alt-right during Trump's first campaign. Former Breitbart editor Ben Shapiro started the hugely popular Daily Wire, and Glenn Beck's TheBlaze mixed more standard conservative fare with "woke" obsessions. There were blogs and sites like Gateway Pundit, and Revolver News. The latter almost single-handedly drove the false narrative that an erratic Trump supporter named Ray Epps was part of a vast plot by federal agents to create the Capitol riot and frame honest, peace-loving Americans.[13]

Even further to the right – and perhaps the true heir to the more extreme factions of the alt-right – was white nationalist podcaster Nick Fuentes, who consistently embraced Nazism, incel culture and racial slurs while hunkered down in his home in a suburb of Chicago.[14] Fuentes, who was present at the Capitol on January 6, 2021, championed himself as leader of the Groypers, a hardcore movement of sexually stunted young men dedicated to embarrassing alt-righters who even countenanced engaging with mainstream conservativism.

It's almost impossible to see how the Groypers could turn into a political movement with any viability whatsoever, but that wasn't the point – the point was getting attention, which they managed to do, sometimes with ease. Fuentes was associated with the quixotic presidential campaign of Kanye West and arranged a bizarre interview of the hip hop superstar by Alex Jones in December 2022. West, wearing a full face mask, praised Hitler and Nazis. Even Jones found it a bit too spicy to handle. If the Infowars boss presented an ideological test, Fuentes and the Groypers posed a much tougher one – were you someone who tolerated Fuentes in the name of free speech, or did you disavow his incel fascism? In the world of fringe right podcasting, this question was the subject of much more debate than you might expect.

No list of self-declared contrarians would be complete without the world's most popular podcaster, Joe Rogan. Rogan[15] falls into the category of people whose political history and background could certainly not be classified as far-right. He has long professed a mix of political views, and his MO of mostly letting people talk, at tremendous length, without much in the way of difficult questioning, has been lightly applied to guests of all sorts. Notably, he supported Bernie Sanders in 2020 and had Sanders on his show, a fact that is brought up repeatedly by his defenders.[16]

But several years into a bumper deal with the world's leading music streaming service, Rogan increasingly seemed to fall into agreement with a range of his increasingly fringe guests over increasingly fringe issues. He has a track record of calling being transgender a mental illness, spreading Covid-19-related misinformation and anti-vaccine propaganda, asserting as fact that the federal government was behind the Capitol riot, calling Jewish people greedy and referring to other anti-Semitic tropes, and of course arguing that "Alex Jones was right about a lot of stuff."[17] Rogan's professed free thinking has, perhaps ironically, fallen into a predictable pattern, one laid out by the conspiratorial far right.

The reaction to this anti-progressive bloc from more establishment conservatives has been significantly different than the response to the nascent alt-right in 2015 and 2016. Back then, click-fishing outbursts by the biggest stars of the alt-right were often greeted with horror by moderate conservatives. And the ill feeling was mutual.

But just as Trump has pushed his opponents within the Republican Party to the fringes, newer influencers have experienced relatively less pushback from the existing establishment. It might be that the idea of "no enemies to the right" – and the fact that conservatives fear being shut out of power – mean that even those closest to the center ground are freaking out about being permanently cast aside. Or perhaps they are caught by some of their own rhetoric, and dare not air their opposition in public for fear of encouraging "cancel culture."

My visit to Alex Jones' estate came a few years after I had visited what was once one of the bellwethers of the right wing, Glenn Beck's TheBlaze. Beck was an original anti-progressive, explicitly so, once saying on his radio show: "To the day I die I am going to be a progressive-hunter."[18] On his Fox News show, he spread conspiracy theories about Barack Obama.

TheBlaze, which Beck started in 2011, was headquartered in a cavernous building outside of Dallas, with full-size studio sets and proper lighting – it looked more a well-funded TV network than an upstart social media operation.

Our visit came deep in the white-hot heat of the 2016 election, and its purpose was not to interview Beck, but one of his protégés, Tomi Lahren. After a sometimes combative interview with Lahren, whose machine-gun rants were lighting up social media, we were about to leave the building when one of

Beck's assistants ran up and offered us an impromptu tour of his boss' "vault."

At first glance, the vault did not exactly live up to its name – rather than a shadowy space behind a heavy metal door, the memorabilia were haphazardly laid out around a bright, cluttered office. There were several eras worth of weaponry and armor – with a heavy emphasis on materiel from both sides of both World Wars – an electric chair, rare copies of the Bible, and somewhat incongruously, lots of Disney-related artifacts. My colleague couldn't quite contain her astonishment at the bizarreness of the whole place.

Beck himself was undergoing something of a rehabilitation at the time, having not long before told *The New Yorker* that Donald Trump was "dangerously unhinged," that he had sympathy with the Black Lives Matter movement and that Obama's presidency had left him a changed man.[19] He certainly never became a fan of progressivism, but in the heyday of the alt-right, he was trying to put clear water between his movement and the more extreme fringes.

It turned out that not even a conservative of Beck's clout and experience could escape the gravitational pull of the conspiracy tendency.

In 2022, both Glenn Beck and Alex Jones came out with books titled *The Great Reset*.[20] Both were attempted takedowns of the World Economic Forum's plan, the one that conspiracists saw as a communist takeover instigated by the world's leading capitalists.[21]

"I absolutely believe they are planning an enormous assault on our freedoms," Jones writes, "and we must figure out the best way to counter their designs."

In his book, Beck[22] argued that "the United States – and indeed the entirety of Western civilization – is in grave peril because of the Great Reset. Only strong resistance from those who believe in democratic principles and individual liberty can stop it."

Two of the most influential men on the right-wing fringes had taken very different paths in reaction to Trump and the alt-right. But as the world emerged from the Covid pandemic and America faced its new future, the fringes had become mainstream and the lines between right and far-right were rapidly disappearing. And both Glenn Beck and Alex Jones had ended up in exactly the same place.

There is a term that has become fashionable to describe the way in which online activists and influencers can inspire violent events: stochastic terrorism. This is the idea that hate speech increases the likelihood of violent attacks, but in an unpredictable and seemingly random way.[23] It's a somewhat knotty theory, as the effects of speech are difficult to trace precisely. Of course, those accused of encouraging stochastic terrorism wholly reject the claim. But on the other hand, words do matter; the anti-progressives know and believe this, as evidenced by their prodigious output. It's clear that words do have an impact, and sometimes – particularly in a large, heavily armed country where millions suffer with mental health problems – a profoundly negative one.

There are a large number of examples of far-right influencers holding sway over people who went on to commit terrible attacks, but I'll outline one case that I examined closely.

In October 2023, in Plainfield, Illinois, about an hour outside of Chicago, a 71-year-old man who had been listening to conservative talk radio and who was worried about attacks on the power grid flew into a paranoid frenzy. Police said that he was motivated by hate and the conflict in the Middle East, which had exploded again a week prior, and that he repeatedly stabbed his lodgers, a Palestinian immigrant and her American-born six-year-old son. The mother lived; the boy, Wadea al-Fayoume, reportedly told her "Mom, I'm fine" before he died from his wounds.[24]

Two days later, I went to the boy's funeral, at a mosque in a suburban area known as Little Palestine. The huge crowd was distraught, anxious, shocked and spinning with grief. They held their camera phones aloft as the boy's small coffin was loaded into the back of a car. Several of them told me the alleged murderer was poisoned by an atmosphere of disinformation and suspicion directed at Palestinians. They blamed the US government, their leaders and the media. They were specifically riled up by reports that Hamas militants had beheaded children. The rumor, sourced to Israel Defense Force soldiers, started circulating shortly after the attacks began.

It was almost impossible to verify or debunk. But it turned out that there was no real proof that the alleged assailant heard such rumors; nor did he need such gruesome details in order to be spurred to action. There was another telling piece of information that prosecutors revealed in the course of their allegations. Outside of his obsession with events in the Middle East and fears about the downfall of the US power grid, the attacker had been worried about a "National Day of Jihad."

That idea stemmed from a statement made by a former Hamas leader, who told Muslims to "head to the squares and streets of the Arab and Islamic world on Friday" to protest in support of Palestinians. He called for countries neighboring Israel to join the fight.[25]

This filtered down through far-right influencer networks, where it was interpreted as a call for murder and terror attacks inside the United States. Several prominent right-wingers – including "DC Draino," Marjorie Taylor Greene and Charlie Kirk – posted messages saying they would prepare with guns and ammo.[26] Law enforcement agencies including the FBI said they were on a heightened state of alert, although they had no specific credible threats. The messages reached a man in

Illinois who had once been on friendly terms with his Palestinian tenants. He became convinced, prosecutors said, that people were coming to attack him, and he lashed out and killed a small boy.[27]

"Conspiracy was always a part of Infowars," Kelly Jones told me as the light began to fade on the plaster circus animals dotted around the yard, back on that evening in late 2018. "But it became more of a part, and more outrageous. He saw he could get attention by doing these outrageous things."

Kelly Jones rued what she had helped create, and what it had become.

But all those heaps of attention that had been collected day in and day out by all of those influencers and grifters on the anti-progressive fringes weren't just numbers on a social network graph or an easy way to turn clicks into nutritional supplement sales.

The ideas they were spreading were worming their way into the brains of millions, all over the country. They were now affecting people who had never listened to Infowars, who didn't spend hours a day on X/Twitter or listening to fringe podcasts. In a measure of just how pervasive some of these ideas have become, some of the people who talked about these ideas now claimed they were common sense, and that they themselves were not into politics at all. And as I traveled around the country, I increasingly encountered the effects of all of these torrents of content, how they were pushing into the mainstream, and how the messages of the far-right, anti-progressive influencers were reaching into every corner of the United States.

10
Revenge of the normies

It's hard to imagine a place more middle America than Indianola, Iowa. Take its geographic position for starters – Iowa is in the middle of the country, Warren County is in the middle of Iowa, and Indianola, the county seat and largest town, is right in the middle of that.

And right in the middle of Indianola is a square, laid out around a county courthouse, lined with coffee shops and small stores, a soda fountain selling penny candy with a soda jerk slinging brightly colored phosphates alongside coffee and tea. Just north of downtown are the brick buildings of Simpson College clustered around a football field, surrounded by residential neighborhoods of sturdy Midwestern houses laid out on arrow-straight grid-like streets, and beyond that lies the everywhere sprawl – motels, gas stations, fast-food outlets, a Wal-Mart. Indianola is a microcosm of the United States.

Every four years over the past few decades, Iowa becomes the center of American political life due to the state's first-in-the-nation presidential contests. But when I drove into town the day after Independence Day in 2023, I was in search of a very local story – one that demonstrated just how deeply conspiratorial thinking was now baked into the mainstream.

The controversy sprang to life when the Warren County board, comprised of three Republicans, was considering who should replace the last county auditor, who had decided to retire before the end of her term. They passed over the deputy auditor – who, like the retiring auditor, was a Democrat –

in favor of a political neophyte, a Republican named David Whipple.

Although he lacked experience in government, Whipple had had a long and successful business career. But what irked many locals were posts that he had shared online around the time of the 2020 presidential election.

One was a link to a QAnon documentary. "The line in the sand is near," he wrote.

Another of his posts pointed to a 9/11 conspiracy documentary. He commented: "U better watch this."

And there was election denial. Whipple was a Republican and a supporter of Donald Trump. On November 6, 2020, he shared a post that cited debunked statistics: "How did Minnesota have 5,149,039 votes when they only have 3,588,563 registered voters???"

Three days later, he commented: "Joe admits MASSIVE VOTER FRAUD during brain fart. SHARE before fb takes it down!"

By the time he was appointed auditor of Warren County, David Whipple told me, he had left election conspiracies behind. Even if there was some voter fraud, in a land somewhere beyond Iowa, he said he now believed that Joe Biden was the legitimately elected president of the United States.

After a crushing handshake, Dave ushered me into his office and showed me the piles of paperwork and binders lined up behind his desk. He wore a bright blue short-sleeved shirt, a pair of wire-framed glasses looped into the collar, and he apologized for having only a lunchtime half-hour to chat. He was very busy reforming the auditor's office, he said, before admitting that yes, he'd got carried away by his fealty towards Donald Trump.

"It was a very emotional time for a lot of people in the world," he said. "There was smoke, and where there's smoke, you have got to see if there's fire."

Whipple's Facebook posts became a public issue after he was appointed, and initially I had assumed that nobody outside of his friends and family had known about them before he was named to public office. On that, I was wrong.

Later that day, I visited Kedron Bardwell, a political science professor at Simpson College, as he was working in his office on the nearly deserted campus. Among other things, Bardwell teaches classes on misinformation and conspiracy theories. Bardwell has a keen interest in politics at all levels, and he was the one who first brought Whipple's posts to public attention.

"I emailed one of the county supervisors immediately after the appointment happened, and I said, 'Have you seen these posts? Did you know what you're doing?'" he said.

A member of the county board, Mark Snell, initially tried to call the kettle black, saying that reporting on Dave Whipple's posts was a "misinformation campaign." He later told a local newspaper that they were, instead, "inconsequential" and "benign."[1]

The board had known about the posts, but they didn't see the problem. In fact, Snell told reporters:[2] "I could see myself liking those (posts) because at the time, during the election last fall, there were a lot of allegations."

David Whipple's past forays into conspiracy world weren't just excusable errors – among the local Republican establishment, they were completely, utterly normal.

Again and again in my coverage of politics both subterranean and surface-level, I noticed a pattern. Election denial and related conspiracy theories were having an unusual, uneven impact across the country. In some places – politically mixed or Democrat-leaning – they were a hindrance and were costing Republicans votes. The impact of this could be seen during the 2022 midterm elections, when Republicans underperformed, including in several races where the party primaries had selected fringe candidates over more mainstream ones.

But among Trump loyalists, and in parts of the country where Republicans ruled, conspiratorial thinking was rarely frowned upon; in fact, it was often celebrated.

Having been thwarted in their top-down attempted takeover on January 6, 2021, election deniers were now trying to take power from the bottom up. They showed up at local council meetings across the country[3] and supported school board members in places like Sarasota.[4] Going local was a conscious choice, encouraged by influencers like Steve Bannon, Proud Boys and others.

And they were winning – being voted into all sorts of other positions of minor civic power, like county auditors, that collectively make up the space where much of the day-to-day governance of the United States happens.[5]

Because many conservative activists believed that voting was corrupt, they were particularly interested in positions that had control over elections. Prior to the 2022 midterm elections, one such effort emerged from allies of a QAnon influencer.

This bizarre story started in Nevada, with a businessman named Jim Marchant. Marchant[6] ran for Congress in 2020, and like Trump, he lost. Also like Trump, he blamed his loss on vote fraud and dirty tricks. In fact, Marchant went even further than Trump, claiming that all Nevada elections all the way back to 2006 were rigged, with elected officials installed by a "deep state cabal."

With the help of a QAnon influencer who goes by the pseudonym "Juan O Savin" – a faux-Spanish garbling[7] of the pronunciation of the number "107" – Marchant organized a group of seven candidates called the America First Secretary of State Coalition.

The job of state secretary of state is almost as obscure as that of county auditor. In some states the position is elected, in others it is appointed. The exact responsibilities of the post vary. Unlike the US Secretary of State, state secretaries of state have nothing to do with foreign policy. In most states, this person instead controls licensing and business regulations.

But in many states, the secretary of state also serves as the top election official, and that's why Marchant and other fringe Republicans were suddenly interested in the job.[8]

The America First Secretary of State Coalition was explicit about its goals – elimination of mail-in and electronic ballots and "aggressive voter roll clean-up." It listed its other aims on its website: "Voter Integrity," which it believed had been completely lost, and to "Counter and Reverse electoral fraud," which it believed was rampant.[9]

When Trump held a rally in Nevada in October 2022, the former president called Jim Marchant onto the stage. Marchant seized the opportunity to hammer home the central theme of his campaign.

"We have something in common," he told the crowd. "President Trump and I both lost an election in 2020 because of a rigged election."

Although it had high-profile support, from Trump on down, and included one of Trump's most prominent allies, Kari Lake of Arizona,[10] the America First Secretary of State Coalition failed. All but one of its candidates lost.

The rebuke to the denialists was part of that larger pattern across the country. In many close districts, denialism turned out to be a bad electoral strategy. The worst worries of the pundits – widespread January 6-style violence following the 2022 midterms – did not come to pass. But conspiratorial narratives remained, and in some cases, were as powerful as ever.[11]

And, somewhat counterintuitively, the results of those mid-terms strengthened the hand of election deniers in Congress. Kevin McCarthy, the Speaker of the House, was forced to rely on – and give concessions to – far-right members, including the House Freedom Caucus. They would not be placated, however; the pact doomed his speakership within a year.

Like the Trump administration, the Freedom Caucus itself turned out to be much better at rhetorical bomb-throwing than the slog of governing, and susceptible to paranoia. By mid-2023, it was beset by infighting and had ousted its best-known member, Marjorie Taylor Greene.[12] The split seemed more about personality clashes than any member dissenting from the right-wing orthodoxy about supposed Democrat pedophile rings and peacefulness of the Capitol rioters.[13]

Some Freedom Caucus members did, at least briefly, break with Trump to endorse other candidates during the Republican primary. But they remained united behind the idea that a deep state conspiracy was actively working to shut down the most extreme right-wing members of Congress. A fractious hearing with FBI director Christopher Wray in July 2023 demonstrated the alternative reality that several lawmakers – emboldened by their constituents all across the country – had embraced. The accusations from the most conservative members of Congress piled up fast. The agency was spying on American citizens simply because they had been at the Capitol in January 2021. It was censoring conservatives on social media. Freedom Caucus member Chip Roy called the FBI "tyrannical." Congressman Jim Jordan proposed moving the agency from Washington to Alabama, where he posited it would be free of political interference, or, one supposes, free of one particular type of political interference.

Flabbergasted Democrats called the hearing "bananas," among other things, but the minority had little power to halt proceedings. Wray, who seemed to want to talk more about the dangers of fentanyl, China and mass shooters, protested that he was a Republican himself and had zero motivation to censor conservatives. His pleas went mostly unheard. The hearing demonstrated the power of the idea that the system was completely stacked against the right – by which the Freedom Caucus meant the fringe right, its own particular brand of scorched-earth MAGA extremism.

It does not take very long, once you land in the United States, to realize that quite radical ideas that would be astonishing in other contexts can easily be wrapped in trappings of normal American life. With the exception of only the most extreme far-right groups, those on the fringes cover themselves in the flag and present themselves as the true representatives of average, everyday Americans, defending their supposedly mainstream values against the threat of the moment.

I saw this firsthand in Portland, a few days after my encounter with Edie Dixon. Our crew was invited to a Proud Boys gathering. It was more of a party than an official meeting, with a couple of dozen members in a tidy suburban house. Some played first-person shooter video games in the living room under a framed American flag honoring a veteran. It was the kind of thing I'd seen in the houses of friends and relatives all over the country.

Our host, who was cagey about appearing on camera, worked for a government contractor. One of the Proud Boys had barbecued some ribs, and all the men were pounding copious amounts of light beer.

In the garage, some of the Proud Boys puffed on joints and cigarettes and looked on as others availed themselves of a makeshift gym. It was an authentic American scene, one that could have played out nearly anywhere in the country, and yet these men wore T-shirts with slogans praising fascist dictators and regularly took to the streets to batter their political opponents.

One of them, Tiny Toese, was the de facto leader of their band of brothers. The nickname "Tiny" was a euphemism. He was an enormous man and could hoick up the heaviest bundles of the weights in the garage. Tiny was not only the strongest Proud Boy in the Portland group, but one of the youngest – in his early twenties at the time, among a group of men mostly in their thirties and older.

Tiny had moved to the mainland United States a few years previously from his home in American Samoa. He had worked hard at several jobs and believed in the elusive American dream. Something about what he saw as the ungratefulness of left-wing Portlanders had triggered him, and he'd fallen in with the Proud Boys and a local Christian nationalist group, Patriot Prayer, often acting as a bodyguard at their rallies, which just as often descended into violent clashes. Still, like the rest of the Proud Boys, he insisted that the group was just a misunderstood social club.

"Most guys are just here for the drinking," he told me as wafts of smoke danced in front of our camera. The anti-fascists, he continued, were "being selfish."

"Not everybody in Portland agrees with them. And if they're trying to build a community, it's a community of masked ninjas that does not follow the law."

Somewhat ironically, he told us about all the times he'd been arrested. The total number, he reckoned, was 18.

On Portland's streets, Tiny thumped counter-protesters and got into a fight with a teenager at a mall. He was pictured at rallies wearing a "Right Wing Death Squad" patch and a T-shirt that referenced Augusto Pinochet: "MAKE COM-MUNISTS AFRAID OF ROTARY AIRCRAFT AGAIN" it said over a drawing of stick figures with antifa-flag heads being dropped from the sky. "PHYSICAL REMOVAL SINCE 1973."[14]

Tiny traveled around the country with the Proud Boys, too, often in violation of bail terms placed on him by Portland judges. He was seen at protests in Texas after Alex Jones was removed from major social media platforms, and in Seattle when anarchist activists took over a chunk of the city after police abandoned one of their stations.

He was a regular participant in the daily street battles that roiled the city in 2020. And as Donald Trump was defeated and left office, Tiny and the rest of the Portland area Proud Boys continued to get involved in extremist violence. In August 2021, he was involved in a paintball and pepper spray shootout with anti-fascists, which also involved smashing up a van. The following month, he was reportedly shot in the ankle in Olympia, Washington State.

I marveled at his ability to avoid long jail terms, but his streak of luck ran out in 2023 when he was handed a sentence of nearly eight years in prison for assault, riot and weapons charges.[15]

In that makeshift garage gym, Tiny contended that the violence was always and in every case justified as self-defense. He and his boys were on the side of law and order, he insisted. The anti-fascists were the lawless ones.

"We got tired of people getting beat up," he told me, "just because they have a different belief from the people who are running around with masks."

The Proud Boys thought they were protecting their homes and families and American values from what they thought were evil leftist communists. They were willing to accept people who were a little different as long as they thought like them and were willing to fight. They truly believed that, were it not for the malign forces that the deep state or local authorities were unwilling to root out, they wouldn't have to get involved in politics at all, and would simply be left in peace with their beer and barbecue.

But as a group, they resonated with the broader paranoia on the far right. They thought they were in a battle for the soul of their country, and it sometimes made them crazy with rage. Their image of themselves as pure defenders of American values, acting righteously, wasn't just a front for the camera. It was part of their very deepest beliefs.

One more person stuck in my mind from my first year back in my native country, not for his membership of an extreme group or political ambitions, but for his remarkable normality.

I met Donny outside the airport in West Palm Beach while we waited for Donald Trump's private plane to take off for New York.

It was April 2023, and Trump was facing the first in a series of criminal indictments on various charges in various jurisdictions.

Donny is a very large, affable man, originally from Phila-delphia, who now lives in Fort Myers, about three hours to the west of Trump's Mar-a-Lago estate. On that warm April day, he was wearing a large white shirt that rippled in the breeze. He toted an American flag as he walked up and down a small spit of grass that separates US Highway 98 from Palm Beach airport.

"All elected officials are corrupt," he told me, as we chatted underneath a banner printed with the QAnon slogan "TRUST THE PLAN." The crowd of a couple of hundred people around us included retirees decked out in red, white and blue shirts and shorts, a family on vacation from Ohio, a Cuban émigré, and a woman who'd had too much to drink and paused long enough to tell me "The mainstream media lies about vaccines and everything" before stomping back to her cooler full of beer.

Donny was chatty and clearly not drunk or crazy. Trump, he told me, was a different kind of person.

"He's an easy target, he opens his mouth, he's rich, and he's less of a politician than any politician out there," he said.

He pressed two copies of a book that he had written into my hand. I thanked him, and later I flicked through a copy. It was a 300-page stream-of-extremely-online-consciousness which touched on everything from voting fraud to vaccines to the history of the Democratic Party and the secrets of elite corruption at the highest levels. It included copious citations of news articles and, at points, transcriptions of videos and biographical details pasted from websites.

It was a sprawling, confusing text, but if I had to sum it up, Donny's thesis is that there are evil, hateful people in charge of the country, have always been in charge of the country, and they are masters at dividing up the population and screwing ordinary Americans. His argument was backed up by conspiratorial thinking and weird interpretations of history, but on one level it made a certain sort of sense. It was the Trump argument – at least, the Trump argument which got him elected in 2016. Donny may not have been its most fluent messenger, but it was the kind of message that resonated with millions of Americans, of many different political stripes.

In conspiracy world there are thousands of people with self-published books like Donny's, and millions more with Facebook, YouTube and Twitter accounts, aspiring influencers who are convinced that the truth is being hidden from them and willing to attach their support to someone, anyone, who can lead the country out of the abyss.

A decade ago, I produced a radio series focusing on homegrown US extremists.[16] It included interviews with Islamist propagandists, a gun-toting neo-Nazi on a porch in Idaho, an odd gentleman who ran a quixotic organization dedicated to re-segregating Alabama, and many others. They sometimes seemed like stock characters, baddies from the movies. But in the ten years since, I watched as the energy of the fringes moved online, attached to Trump, went mainstream.

The far right could no longer be ignored. Their ideas were now being adopted by millions of ordinary people, folks you might bump into on the street, anywhere in America. Including people like Donny.

Back in Iowa, David Whipple told me that even though he had moved on from his anger after the 2020 election, his suspicions around America's voting system lingered. Not only did he still wonder if election fraud had happened in faraway cities, he said, he had even heard rumors of underhanded activity closer to home.

"People come up to me all the time that are former employees, they're ex-poll workers, there's some issues that have been happening," he told me.

The potential problems, he elaborated, were that some poll watchers had been told they weren't allowed in certain areas on election days, that some people said they were being issued different ballots depending on whether they were registered Republican or Democrat, and that some poll workers had changed their party registration shortly before an election, only to switch it back again after.

"Whether or not these things are true, I don't know, because personally, I didn't witness them myself," he admitted. He repeated the metaphor he had used before, about the 2020 election. "But it makes me think there's smoke here. So let me go investigate the fire."

It later occurred to me that Whipple might have been confused by the difference between poll workers – non-partisan volunteers who help administer elections – and poll watchers, political partisans who watch the poll workers. Political parties also hand out voting guides, sometimes referred to as "sample ballots," listing their endorsed candidates, crib sheets for voters as they head to the polls.

Bardwell, local journalists and others in Indianola told me that any allegations of widespread voter fraud in Warren County were preposterous. The most controversial election day snafu in recent years happened when a volunteer prematurely yanked a thumb drive out of its slot. It ended the electronic count, and poll workers instead tallied paper ballots. There was no hint that voting shenanigans were happening on any noticeable scale or that IT issues or anything else had corrupted election results. And if there was some sort of grand plan to fix elections, it hadn't exactly worked. In a place that was once fairly evenly divided, there were now no county-wide elected Democrats. The county, like the rest of the state, had been steadily trending towards Republicans for years. Local Democrats ascribed their recent failures to the shifting national and state political mood – not fraud.

But Whipple's suspicions – combined with his previous spreading of conspiracy theories and the particular attention lavished on a special election – proved to be a few steps too far for voters in Warren County. When a recall petition resulted in a vote in late August 2023, Whipple lost 66 percent to 33 percent, in a county that Donald Trump had won by 17 percentage points three years earlier. He had been in office less than three months.

The result did not move the local Republican leadership to change tack. Like Whipple, they still harbored suspicions, if not about the overwhelming result of the auditor's race, then about voting procedures in general. There had been irregularities found in the auditor's office, they said. Thumb drives were unsecured and voting machines were suspiciously unmonitored. There was ample evidence of best-practice procedures not followed. They believed that the voting system was shot through with corruption and mismanagement, and that their attempts at what they thought were common-sense reforms were being stymied by elites – the Democratic Party, liberal local journalists and now, the international media. Those were the lessons they took from Whipple's defeat.

Ironically, on a national scale, insistence on the Big Lie tended to hold back any significant changes to the voting system, as it had the effect of making Democrats dig in their heels even about relatively uncontroversial changes to the voting system. But then again, small changes were not what the new far right was aiming for. It was a movement that dove full speed ahead into the 2024 presidential contest with a much, much grander vision of revolution on its mind.

Conclusion: Day of reckoning

A few weeks after I visited Warren County, I drove due west from Chicago with my family to visit some friends in eastern Iowa. Jackson County bumps up against the Mississippi River and is much hillier than you would expect it to be. It's an agricultural area, and as we got closer to the county fair, I tuned the radio into the only station I could find, which was broadcasting a live cattle auction.

The fair was replete with 4H (Head, Heart, Hands and Health) displays, animal shows, carnival rides and permutations of fried food. Politics was only a small part of the menu. A few fairgoers wore red MAGA hats, and a loquacious farmer in a checked shirt overseeing the goat petting enclosure proudly declared that he'd voted for Trump once, but never would again. The weather was sweltering, like it was in so much of North America in the summer of 2023. Inside a thankfully air-conditioned building, stuffed with the winners of the vegetable, baking, place-setting and craft-making competitions, were stalls run by political parties. I picked up a copy of the Iowa Republican Party platform.

It began with standard, predictable Republican Party ideas – a ban on abortion, encouragement of free markets, an end to things like gun control and Obamacare and so on.

But as I read on, I noticed some strange digressions. The Iowa Republicans were looking to eliminate birthright citizenship – the idea that anyone born in the United States is automatically a citizen. It's an idea enshrined in the 14th Amendment, and one that Donald Trump periodically criticizes. The Iowa Republicans were also no fans of the 16th and 17th Amendments (which established income tax and direct election of US Senators, respectively). In contrast, they were fans of the 1st Amendment, citing one particular reason: "to allow prayer in Public Schools and Public Places."

The Republican platform included a ban on public sector unions and a rejection of "any movement toward a government controlled and/or monitored cashless society," a policy proposal taken directly from fevered speculation about the "Great Reset." They demanded an end to government agencies including "the Internal Revenue Service, the Environmental Protection Agency, the Bureau of Alcohol, Tobacco and Firearms, the Transportation Security Administration, the Bureau of Land Management, the Department of Labor and the Department of Education." Also gone, if they had their way, was any teaching on gender identity and sexual orientation, along with any government attempts to combat "alleged man-made global warming."

And:

> The Republican Party of Iowa goes on record as supporting the efforts of the various states (including but not limited to Wisconsin, Michigan, Pennsylvania, Georgia, and Arizona) involved in ongoing legal challenges seeking ultimately to de-certify the 2020 Presidential Election vote due to the findings of massive irregularities and fraud.

These people weren't weird or outliers. This was now the mainstream, another example of how the fringes had taken over, how suspicion of voting systems, theories about the deep state, disinformation about climate change, panic about gender, and paranoid fantasies had burrowed into American life.

It was clear that Donald Trump's campaign and the rise of the alt-right had presaged a shift in American politics, and that, even years later, the former president still commanded the loyalties of millions. And I had long studied online extremism, a wave that had radicalized young men and sparked violence driven by paranoia and hate.

But somehow, before moving back to the United States, I had underestimated how strong these forces had become. I somehow expected to find a more nuanced picture, more common sense, steady logic, and some sort of innate spirit of moderation, especially in the Midwest. But the lines between the fringes and the mainstream were more than just blurred; they were quickly being erased.

At the same time, the rest of the country was struggling to get a grip on the true nature of the new far right. Perhaps part of the problem was a constant state of alarm during the Trump years along with the constant hope that something – impeachment, an election, death by Covid – would permanently usher him off the political stage. Coverage of Trump's ties to Russia – or to be more specific, social media reaction to coverage of Trump's ties to Russia – itself often veered into the conspiratorial.

The language of identity politics and heartfelt grievances about broad systems were increasingly absorbed into parts of the mainstream media – the major newspapers, public radio, and the CNN/MSNBC side of the cable news divide. In a different filter bubble, mainstream conservatives were themselves often too blinded by culture wars and scared of the potential blowback from policing the fringes to govern their own movement.

At the same time, real change in a country that seemed hungry for it seemed frustratingly, stubbornly slow. Sheer news fatigue was another factor. At the national level, the racist murder spree in Jacksonville, Florida in August 2023 came and went in a ferocious news cycle or two, as did the killing of a California store owner who refused to take down a rainbow flag.[1] And of course, these were fractious times, with conflicts in the Middle East, in Ukraine, tensions with China and countless other stories competing for attention.

Due to some combination of all of these factors, some of the most fascinating and terrifying recent developments in American politics were somehow not the subject of daily debate and discussion.

Conspiracy theorizing can function as an imaginative aid, a type of thinking that offers alternative possibilities about the world and its future.[2] They can be, as a father of a Sandy Hook victim once told me, "mental chewing gum," a moderately pleasurable way to let one's mind drift into other realms. Think about a simpler conspiracy past: the imaginative work which goes into imagining how the Beatles could cover up the death of Paul McCartney, or how the moon landing could have been portrayed on a film set.

But the conspiracy theories that have recently come to prominence are of a different quality. They are explicitly political. Their dark and chaotic dreams are front and center, and in the lead-up to the 2024 election, I found them everywhere I went. Furthermore, conspiracy theories about voting and pedophile cabals were not just addressing politics, but in the minds of their followers they became the whole of politics, filling millions of Americans with hatred and suspicion.

The stress of Covid and the influence of Donald Trump certainly contributed to this phenomenon, but the trend goes back further; rapid social change, inequality and economic stagnation, and social media algorithms all have something to do with it, even as its exact scale and specific contours are still being worked out. There's no sign that the fever is going to break any time soon.

But on the individual level – for the millions of everyday conspiracy theory followers – credulousness can be boiled down fairly simply: they want to believe.

A world without human responsibility for climate change is easier to live in than one with difficult choices and increasingly extreme weather. The world would be a more comfortable place without killers motivated by hatred or white supremacy, so for some it's easier to explain them away. If election conspiracies are true, we can reassure ourselves that our chosen candidate is an unfairly maligned uniter, rather than a divider disliked or loathed by more than half the population. The fear, panic and anger that people felt during the pandemic must have some meaning – and so must be repaid by the punishment of people who urged others to wear masks or get Covid vaccines. QAnon believers long for a world where Trump and his allies lie ready and waiting for the right moment to execute all the pedophiles, because pedophiles are out there, and they are scary.

The conspiracy theory believers want to believe. The alternative – reality – is too much to bear.

In August 2023, as his rivals squared off in the first Republican presidential debate, Donald Trump sloughed off the pack and instead sat for a chummy chat with Tucker Carlson.[3] While others zeroed in on the eight contenders taking the stage in Milwaukee, I waded through more than 45 meandering minutes that showed just how detached MAGA had become from reality. Carlson asserted that Jeffrey Epstein had been murdered, and while Trump allowed for the possibility, he said: "I think he probably committed suicide."

"I'm not a conspiracy person at all," Carlson said. He chuckled and added, jokingly: "I believe everything I hear."

He turned serious again.

"Are you worried they're going to try to kill you?" Carlson asked.

Neither Carlson nor Trump defined the "they," but from context it's clear that they meant the former president's political enemies – maybe Democrats or anti-fascists, maybe prosecutors or Justice Department officials who had lodged the criminal complaints against him.

"They're savage animals, they are people who are sick, really sick," Trump replied. "You have great people in the Democrat Party, you have great people who are Democrats ... but I've seen what they do, I've seen the lengths that they go to."

From assassination, the conversation drifted to even drearier topics. Trump said he would easily end the war in Ukraine and had prevented a nuclear war with North Korea. He rambled about the building of the Panama Canal, electric cars, devices that limit water flow in shower heads ("I ended all of that," he said, almost as an aside), Chinese influence in Latin America, and the electoral votes of Wisconsin, which Trump claimed he'd won in 2020. US elections, he said, should return to paper ballots, with mandatory voter identification, and no early or mail-in voting. Although he didn't mention the group by name, it happened to be exactly the platform of Jim Marchant's America First Secretary of State coalition.

"Isn't that the whole point of [mail-in ballots]," said Carlson, "to cheat?"

"Their policies are so bad that if they didn't cheat, they couldn't get elected," Trump responded.

Carlson ended by asking whether Trump thought civil war was a real possibility.

"I don't know," Trump said. He emphasized again a line he had used on January 6, 2021 – that protesters should "peacefully and patriotically" make their views known. And he gushed about the events of that day. It might have been the biggest crowd he'd every spoken to, he said, more than a million people, and only a few of them were violent.

"There was love and unity. I have never seen such spirit and passion and such love, and I've also never seen, simultaneously and from the same people, such hatred of what they've done to our country."

Again the "they" in this sentence was implied, not specified.

"So do you think it's possible that there's open conflict?" Carlson asked. "We seem to be moving towards something."

"I don't know," Trump said again. "I can say this. There's a level of passion I've never seen and there's a level of hatred I've never seen. And that's probably a bad combination."

At the time of writing, the course of top-level American politics seems like a grim slog towards gerontocracy. Donald Trump has a near unassailable lead in the Republican Party polls, shows no sign of pulling out despite multiple criminal indictments, and only an astonishing development will prevent him from becoming the party's nominee. Several of his vanquished rivals shared Trump's conspiratorial mindset. Florida Governor Ron DeSantis made opposition to Covid vaccines a key part of his strategy for governing Florida and tried to run to the right of Trump on issues like abortion, trans rights, book bans, education, and "wokeism." Another, Vivek Ramaswamy, pulled out of the race shortly after the Iowa caucuses and endorsed Trump. On the campaign trail, he said things like: "I think it is legitimate to say how many police, how many federal agents, were on the planes that hit the Twin Towers."[4] In Iowa, as Trump steadily solidified his position in the primary contest, these three candidates together collected about 80 percent of the vote.[5] There did not appear to be any non-conspiratorial majority within the Republican Party.

Joe Biden's path to re-nomination will only be derailed by a major development. There is plenty of peril for the president. Third-party and independent challenges abound – from Robert F. Kennedy Jr., progressive Cornel West, the centrist "No Labels" organization, as well as the traditional Green and Libertarian Parties – although whether collectively these will affect Democrats or Republicans more is still up for debate.[6] More specifically, Biden could suffer health problems, or decide – like many voters and pundits already have – that he's too old to run again.

While Trump's grip over the Republican Party seems solid, he also faces a number of hurdles in his quest to retake the White House. His election conspiracy theories are popular with his base, but not the general public. They also have the effect of dissuading his supporters from voting early, by mail, or even at all, because his supporters lack faith in the system. This so worries the Republican Party that in 2023 they started an initiative called "Bank Your Vote"[7] to encourage early voting. The backlash effect of the criminal indictments against him – providing him with huge boosts in attention and particularly in fundraising – appears to be wearing off, according to his campaign finance records. This could be an early sign that the criminal cases, which will be heavily covered throughout 2024, could eventually weigh down his popularity – but perhaps this is again more wishful thinking about a deus ex machina that will whisk him off the political stage.

Perhaps more importantly, the lawsuits could create a campaign money crunch that will hurt him further down the line, preventing him from blasting out ads in Wisconsin, Arizona, Georgia and other marginal states. And, in an interesting twist, quite possibly driven in part by opposition to vaccination, Republicans are dying of Covid at greater rates than Democrats.[8] This "red death" effect is not enormous, but by all accounts the 2024 election will be close. Wisconsin, the tipping point state in the 2020 and 2016 elections,[9] was decided last time by around 20,000 votes, and last time around more than 50,000 Wisconsinites chose someone other than the main two candidates.

If indeed the 2024 election does end up being a contest between Trump and Biden, there will be many stories written that can be summarized as "Ugh, not again." But in all likelihood it will not be as boring as it first seems. America faces the prospect of a risky, chaotic few months or even years as the paranoia bloc turns its antennae towards the campaign and its aftermath. Three-quarters of Americans think the country is on the wrong track, according to one survey carried out in late 2023. A similar number told the pollsters they believe the future of American democracy is at stake in the 2024 election. And nearly a quarter agreed with the statement: "Because things have gotten so far off track, true American patriots may have to resort to violence in order to save our country." Among Republicans and white evangelical Protestants, that proportion is about a third.[10]

In the event of a clear Trump electoral college victory, it seems very likely that protesters will take to the streets in New York, Chicago, Portland and other major American cities. And it's hard to imagine that Trump or his supporters will respond as magnanimously (or as joke-magnanimously) as he did in 2016, tweeting: "Love the fact that the small groups of protesters last night have passion for our great country. We will all come together and be proud!"[11]

Primed for conflict and stoked by their influencers, armed groups could come out to protect businesses from any rioters and confront anti-Trump protesters. It's possible that the president-elect, having escaped the prospect of further criminal proceedings (politically, if not strictly legally), will forget about settling scores, attempt to settle the crowds and quell the violence. But he also might be turbocharged by his personal sense of grievance. As always with Trump, it's hard to exactly tell what he might do. After taking office, he might even follow through on his promises to pardon the Capitol rioters, even the most serious offenders,[12] releasing Oath Keepers, Proud Boys and hundreds of others. They would be greeted with a hero's welcome by the far right.

A second Trump term might follow the lines of the first one – bold statements, attempts to dismantle the so-called "deep state," pushbacks from administrators, appointees, and local and state government officials. Who he chooses to join him in the White House will be telling. Would Mike Flynn or Steve Bannon really be welcomed back? He has already outlined a key part of his plan – the creation of a special class of civil servants who can be hired and fired by the president.[13] It is the first step in cleaning out government bureaucracy, a real attack on the "deep state" that would potentially clear the decks for a wide variety of other radical policies.

Some factions of the far right will embrace him, others – and for sure the hardest of the hardcore – will denounce him for not going far enough. It's also a distinct possibility that regular street fighting between far-right groups and antifa forces will return with a vengeance in cities like Portland and Seattle.

If Trump loses, it's difficult to see a scenario where he and his supporters will go gentle into that good night.

A second Capitol riot, seeking to stop the counting of electoral votes, seems unlikely – after all, it didn't work the first time. But it's also hard to imagine that MAGA would back down without a fight – maybe even a literal one. Who knows what could happen – a blockade in Wisconsin? An armed rally in Arizona? Statehouses in key battlegrounds could become protest targets, as they were on January 6, 2021, in events that were almost entirely overshadowed by the drama in Washington.[14]

Once pro-Trump protesters, some of them armed, start gathering on American streets, the options become chaotic, frightening and potentially deadly. At some point, their leaders will have to make a choice about what they think the events of the past few years have really meant. Since the Capitol riot, many have tried to portray the events of that day as mostly peaceful, with isolated outbreaks of violence, excused by police inaction and/or made worse by police action. Faced with a situation similar to 2020, would the far-right fringes, backed up by an untold number of conservatives and Republicans, make some more noise, smash some more windows, then go home when told to by police? Or would they stay and fight?

An even darker mood could take hold, the one expressed by Stewart Rhodes when he rued not bringing guns to the Capitol: "We should have fixed it right then and there." This current has been running underneath and alongside the spin about how the Capitol riot was actually a peaceful political protest. Their logic is that January 6 was peaceful – but it shouldn't have been. This argument urges the rebels to stand their ground, not give an inch, and be prepared to fight, because violence is the only language their opponents will understand. This drumbeat is getting stronger, even a year out from the election, on social media accounts and fringe podcasts, reflected in Trump and Carlson's talk of assassination and civil war.

The fringe forces that have largely swung behind Trump again won't necessarily see a loss even if the former president's campaign peters out, or he loses, or election denial ends with a shocking armed confrontation on, say, the streets of Madison, Wisconsin. In some ways, a failure to get Trump back into the White House emboldens them further – in the same way the alt-right arguably would have been energized and unified by a Hillary Clinton presidency.

The new far right can contend they were cheated (again) and rail against an increasingly frail Joe Biden, imagining all sorts of nefarious people propping up the administration of the oldest president ever. In the short term, it might seem like the conspiracy theorists have been beaten back to the margins, but they will continue to lash out in ever more bizarre and violent ways. "Lone wolves" will continue to spring out of the morass of 4chan and 8kun and extremist Telegram channels, creating more killers, while the far-right influencer class will have a steady stream of daily outrage to pump out on their podcasts and social media feeds. Violent political attacks will likely continue to be a feature of American life no matter what happens in the election. The United States is in for an uneasy four years – and perhaps longer. And for those who are really at the very fringes – the remnants of the alt-right and the underground accelerationists – instability isn't just a welcome side effect. The chaos itself is the point.

In the normal political world, this all might sound depressing, hopeless even. But the opponents of the far right have crucial tactical advantages: in communities that find reactionary ideas strange and abhorrent, in a high level of motivation to fight back, and in the internal weakness of the fringes, where paranoia and infighting often lead to implosion.

In the autumn of 2022, after my conversations with Dakota Adams, I made one last stop before leaving Montana. It was one week before the midterm elections and one month before Stewart Rhodes would be convicted for his role in the Capitol riot. My destination was the office of Tanya Gersh, who lives and works in Whitefish.

Gersh is a local real estate agent who played a crucial role in marginalizing two of the most noteworthy figures of the alt-right. She is an unlikely main character. Before 2016, she told me, she was not very involved in politics.

"I literally never turned on the news once I left high school," she said. "I was a very happy Jewish person who was always embraced for being a little bit different."

But after the election of Donald Trump, she and millions of others suddenly became aware of the alt-right leader Richard Spencer, the white nationalist who both spearheaded the hardcore alt-right and, with his family fortune and tailored suits, gave it a glossy image miles apart from those white-sheeted rednecks of popular imagination.

Gersh saw the infamous video of Spencer leading a crowd of people giving Nazi-like salutes to the president-elect. She also happened to live in the same town as the Spencers. The attention was vexing Whitefish locals, and Gersh reached out to Spencer's mother Sherry, suggesting that one good way to keep the peace would be to divest her real estate holdings in the town and donate to local anti-hate charities. Gersh offered to help, pro bono, and Mrs. Spencer heard her out.

Gersh didn't give it much further thought until several weeks later, when Sherry Spencer posted an online essay – ghost-written, as was revealed later, by her white nationalist son[15] – accusing Gersh of threatening her and conspiring to run her out of town. The unfounded allegations in turn prompted a hate campaign led by one of the most prominent online neo-Nazis at the time, Andrew Anglin.

Anglin was everything that Richard Spencer was not – weird, creepy, ill-groomed, willing to say the fascist stuff out loud and in public on his website, The Daily Stormer. He launched a campaign of harassment and threatened to send thousands of armed white nationalists to Whitefish to intimidate Gersh and anyone who dared defend her. The town fought back; the march never materialized.[16] The Daily Stormer was good at trolling, harassment, stoking up fear and online attention, but less effective at mustering a street force. The locals celebrated a victory over the alt-right.

At that point, Tanya Gersh could have returned to her business in a beautiful rustic building near Whitefish's well-preserved old western-style downtown. But she didn't. Instead, she sued, and won $14 million. Anglin disappeared, most likely outside of the US, but Gersh has vowed not to let the matter drop.

"There are two different legal teams right now that are following Andrew Anglin and The Daily Stormer and anyone involved to the ends of the earth, and they will not stop. He will never be a free man."

"I hope his followers are paying attention," she told me. "They are cowards."

Anglin and Spencer, the twin faces of alt-right white supremacy, came under further legal pressure after Charlottesville. The Daily Stormer was dropped by an online security company and was chased around the internet, forced to rely on a series of different shaky hosting venues.

The drama in Whitefish was an example of how a backlash against the far right can both rally popular support and persevere over time. Gersh was continuing to process the consequences of her actions when I spoke to her nearly six years later.

"I'm scared. I would be lying if I didn't tell you that," she told me. "I look over my shoulder all the time. I lock my doors now. I'm very conscientious of my surroundings, I never RSVP to anything online."

We chatted about Kanye West and Alex Jones and her concerns about Elon Musk, who at that point just taken over Twitter. Despite all the stress her experiences had brought to her and her family, Tanya Gersh ended our interview by telling me she was "very optimistic." People were fighting back, she said. Hate could be defeated. The far right could be chased out of town.

"I feel like the United States of America cannot simply be thrown away because of a few bad eggs," she said.

In some ways, it's possible to think of events like this as the real and ongoing American civil war – a cold civil war, where some really consequential political developments are happening. It's taking place at the margins, in places like Whitefish and Trego, or in street fights in Portland, school board meetings in Florida, in arguments over library books and county auditor races in Iowa. Committed activists – even some people who until recently didn't read the news – are fighting against reflexive, conspiratorial thinking, algorithmically boosted and virally spread, which every so often incites young men to commit unspeakably horrific violence.

The far right in America today has constructed a parallel infrastructure and a separate language of paranoia, a system of logic that works to sow doubt on anything that it has deemed progressive or mainstream, democratic or Democratic. They have their own sources of truth and their own journalists who have their own ways of operating, funded by a separate economic ecosystem fueled by merch and socials. It's a movement that has a figurehead in Trump, but which will outlast him, and will be fought against in one way by people like Tanya Gersh, in another way by the protesters and anti-fascists who backed her, and in another way by people like Dakota Adams, in a struggle that will continue until the far-right conspiracy world is beaten back towards the margins, or solidifies its significant foothold in American life to such a point that it will seem ridiculous to even try to differentiate it from "mainstream" political life.

There's a chance you picked up this book thinking that the day of reckoning in the title is November 5, 2024 – the date of the next presidential election.

Or maybe you had in mind January 20, 2025, when, as seems likely, either Joe Biden or Donald Trump will be inaugurated for a second term as president.

Or perhaps you had in mind some unspecified morning in a potential future – when Donald Trump will be sentenced to prison, or when his supporters launch a coup attempt.

But the real day of reckoning is not any of those – or rather, it is not any one of those. It is all of those days and many more imaginary ones.

It's the day when the hot civil war starts, or the mass arrests of QAnon's "storm" begins. It's when Donald Trump conquers the deep state or when the trials of the vaccine pushers end in executions. For the even more extreme elements, the day of reckoning is when non-whites are purged from America or the start of the racial holy war.

It's a concept that has motivated the paranoid, cult followers and far-right leaders for decades, and it's an idea that lives in the minds of millions. The events they anticipate are always just around the corner and require endless vigilance, intense preparation, a state of high alert and, every so often, immediate action. They will come tomorrow, or the day after, or the day after that, and so on and so on.

But this movement, despite its intensity, violence and hatred, also contains the germ of its downfall. Because ultimately, the day of reckoning never quite arrives.

Acknowledgments

I have the privilege of working with an all-star cast of top journalists, producers and editors who are behind many of the stories in this book. I could not have done any of this without their help.

I went to Montana with Chelsea Bailey and Eloise Alanna, and to Sandy Hook and Wolfgang Halbig's house in Florida with Sam Judah. I teamed up with Shayan Sardarizadeh to investigate the Maui wildfires, mass shootings in Texas and Florida, the America First Secretary of State Coalition and countless other stories. Rod MacLeod was my producer and video journalist at the QAnon gathering in Scranton, Pennsylvania. I interviewed Stew Peters in Florida along with Rachel Schraer. I was in Berkeley and Portland with Anisa Subedar and Natalia Zuo, and later returned to talk to the Proud Boys with Natalia and director Linda Sills. I went to London lockdown protests with Marianna Spring. I visited TheBlaze in Dallas with Anna Bressanin. I was at Enrique Tarrio's sentencing in Washington with Maxine Hughes.

My editors in the BBC Washington bureau, colleagues in the BBC North America team and the BBC's wider digital department are a great source of support, advice, editorial oversight and brainpower – they include Ben Bevington, Sarah Shenker, Robin Levinson-King, Boer Deng, Rebecca Seales, Jude Sheerin, Tom Geoghegan and Stewart Millar.

The team at BBC Trending and the BBC disinformation team, now part of BBC Verify, are some of the best colleagues I'll ever have. There are many, many fine journalists – too many to list in full – but I'd like to particularly thank Flora Carmichael, Ed Main, Mukul Devichand and Jeremy Skeet.

Special thanks go to my tireless agent Sarah Such and my editor David Castle, along with everyone at Pluto who had faith in this book.

My family is a constant source of support, encouragement and comfort. This book is dedicated to my two sons and my wife Rachel.

Notes

Note: All URLs cited were accessible at time of writing, January 2024.

1   An encounter at the end of the world

1. For safety reasons I have obscured the location of the home of Dakota Adams and some other personal and identifying details about some of the other sources quoted in this book.

2. Mike Wendling, "The saga of 'Pizzagate': The fake story that shows how conspiracy theories spread," BBC News, December 2, 2016, www.bbc.com/news/blogs-trending-38156985/.

3. Southern Poverty Law Center, "Unraveling 'Unite the Right' conspiracy theories," July 24, 2018, www.splcenter.org/hatewatch/2018/07/24/unraveling-unite-right-conspiracy-theories/.

4. "New Right" has been suggested, but is complicated by the fact that several American conservative political movements have gone by this name over the past century. Plus "new" compared to what?

5. Tina Nguyen and Meredith McGraw, "Trumpworld wants distance from QAnon even as the ex-President winks at it," Politico, July 12, 2021, www.politico.com/news/2021/07/12/trump-world-distance-qanon-499242/.

6. Alex Kaplan, "In his first year of actively posting on Truth Social, Trump amplified QAnon-promoting accounts nearly 500 times," Media Matters for America, May 1, 2023, www.mediamatters.org/qanon-conspiracy-theory/his-first-year-actively-posting-truth-social-trump-amplified-qanon/.

7. Jill Colvin, "Trump reveals he got COVID-19 booster shot; crowd boos him," AP News, December 20, 2021, https://apnews.com/article/coronavirus-pandemic-health-donald-trump-coronavirus-vaccine-74abcd4e6833835f5df445fe2142e22b/.

8. Anti-Defamation League, "White supremacist propaganda soars to all-time high in 2022," August 1, 2023, www.adl.org/resources/report/white-supremacist-propaganda-soars-all-time-high-2022/.

9. One of the most prominent proponents of left-wing accelerationism was the writer Mark Fisher, while a notable right-wing version, a manifesto written by Marc Andreessen, picked up a lot of attention in late 2023. Both strands are unlike the extraordinarily dark visions of accelerationist extremists that I'll discuss later in the book. See: Mark Fisher, *Capitalist Realism: Is There No Alternative?* Winchester, UK: Zero Books, 2009; Marc Andreessen, "The Techno-Optimist Manifesto," October 2023, https://a16z.com/the-techno-optimist-manifesto/.

10. Amanda Terkel, "Trump says he would pardon a 'large portion' of Jan. 6 rioters," NBC News, May 11, 2023, www.nbcnews.com/politics/donald-trump/trump-says-pardon-large-portion-jan-6-rioters-rcna83873/.

11. I attempted to speak to Rhodes via his lawyers and wrote to him in prison, but received no response.

2 *2000 Mules and the long "Big Lie"*

1. The Numbers, "Box office performance for documentary movies in 2022," www.the-numbers.com/market/2022/genre/Documentary.

2. Reuters, "Fact check: Clip of Biden taken out of context to portray him as plotting a voter fraud scheme," October 29, 2020, www.reuters.com/article/uk-fact-check-biden-voter-protection-not/fact-check-clip-of-biden-taken-out-of-context-to-portray-him-as-plotting-a-voter-fraud-scheme-idUSKBN27E2VH/.

3. Monmouth University Polling Institute. "Most say fundamental rights under threat," July 12, 2023. www.monmouth.edu/polling-institute/reports/monmouthpoll_US_062023/.

4. A particularly good example is Ali Swenson, "Fact focus: Gaping holes in the claim of 2K ballot 'mules,'" Associated Press, May 3, 2022, https://apnews.com/article/2022-midterm-elections-covid-technology-health-arizona-e1b49d2311bf900f44fa5c6dac406762/.

5. D'Souza did not respond to my requests for comment, though he has spoken to others and has defended the film at length:

Philip Bump, "Discussing the gaps in '2000 Mules' with Dinesh D'Souza," *Washington Post*, May 17, 2022, www.washingtonpost.com/politics/2022/05/17/discussing-gaps-2000-mules-with-dinesh-dsouza/.

6. Jack Healy and Alexandra Berzon, "Town that inspired debunked voter fraud film braces for election day," *New York Times*, November 5, 2022, www.nytimes.com/2022/11/04/us/arizona-voter-fraud-san-luis.html/.

7. As compared to a margin of more than 3,000 amid higher turnout in 2020, according to Yuma County records at www.yumacountyaz.gov/home/showpublisheddocument/48581/637774122997900000/ and www.yumacountyaz.gov/home/showpublisheddocument/48593/637774124460770000/.

8. Stephan Lewandowsky, Klaus Oberauer and Gilles E. Gignac, "NASA faked the moon landing – therefore, (climate) science is a hoax: An anatomy of the motivated rejection of science," *Psychological Science* 24, no. 5 (March 26, 2013): 622–33, https://doi.org/10.1177/0956797612457686/.

9. BBC World Service, "How influential is a pro-Trump conspiracy theory?", July 19, 2019, www.bbc.co.uk/programmes/w3csyvn2/. Uscinski's research can be found in Joseph E. Uscinski, Adam M. Enders, Casey A. Klofstad, Michelle I. Seelig, Hugo Drochon, Kamal Premaratne and Manohar N. Murthi, "Have beliefs in conspiracy theories increased over time?", *PLoS ONE* 17, no. 7 (July 20, 2022): e0270429, https://doi.org/10.1371/journal.pone.0270429/.

10. Ezra Klein, "Here's the real reason Hillary lost the election," CNBC, June 2, 2017, www.cnbc.com/2017/06/02/why-im-defending-hillary-clinton-commentary.html/.

11. To carry the analogy further, consider how many people continued to dispute the legitimacy of the 2016 result in, say, 2019.

12. Salem Media Group, "*2000 Mules* becomes the most successful political documentary in a decade, seen by 1 million," May 12, 2022, www.businesswire.com/news/home/20220511006114/en/2000-Mules-Becomes-the-Most-Successful-Political-Documentary-in-a-Decade-Seen-by-1-Million/.

13. Dinesh D'Souza (@DineshDSouza), "Stewart Rhodes, founder of the Oath Keepers, joins me to talk about his 18-year sentence for sedition despite never entering the capitol on Jan 6.," June 2, 2023, https://

twitter.com/DineshDSouza/status/1664572572925657089/, archived at https://archive.ph/9jOPi/.

3   The murder excuse ballads

1. I looked them up later. The Red Elephants were an alt-right media group that at one point ran a fairly popular YouTube channel. Matthew Hall, "Allegations of racism dominate local workshop," *Santa Monica Daily Press*, July 20, 2017, https://smdp.com/2017/07/20/ allegations-of-racism-dominate-local-workshop/.

2. The News and Advance, "Heather Heyer autopsy report," December 5, 2018, https://newsadvance.com/news/state/heather-heyer-au- topsy-report/pdf_66cc07e2-a216-54a0-ae0b-ebe652e25ad2.html/.

3. This argument was best encapsulated by Breitbart: "Everyone on the anonymous board hurls the most vicious slurs and stereotypes each other, but like jocks busting each other's balls at the college bar, it's obvious that there's little real hatred present." Allum Bokhari and Milo Yiannopoulos, "An establishment conservative's guide to the alt-right," Breitbart, March 30, 2016, www.breitbart.com/tech/2016/03/29/an-establishment- conservatives-guide-to-the-alt-right/.

4. Anti-Defamation League, "Murder and extremism in the United States in 2022," June 23, 2023, www.adl.org/resources/report/ murder-and-extremism-united-states-2022/.

5. Tom Norton, "Fact check: Tucker Carlson says new evidence clears Derek Chauvin of murder," *Newsweek*, October 23, 2023, www. newsweek.com/tucker-carlson-new-evidence-derek-chauvin- murder-george-floyd-1836953. Carlson said on X/Twitter: "Did [Chauvin] actually murder George Floyd? And the answer is, well, no he didn't murder George Floyd." His evidence for this was a deposition by Amy Sweasy, the local prosecutor who filed the initial third-degree murder charge against police officer Derek Chauvin, before they were upgraded to a more serious first-degree murder charge. Sweasy, citing the ongoing legal case, declined to comment when I contacted her.

6. The allegation appears so regularly that fact-checkers have been repeatedly prompted to debunk it over several years: Associated Press, "George Floyd's autopsy report is not new, does not say he

died of an overdose," August 24, 2023, https://apnews.com/article/fact-check-george-floyd-autopsy-new-892530421961/; Associated Press, "Experts: George Floyd died from knee to neck, not drug overdose," October 21, 2022, https://apnews.com/article/fact-check-george-floyd-kanye-west-police-397984860325/; Reuters Fact Check, "Fact Check – No evidence drug overdose was main cause of death for George Floyd in 2020," November 8, 2022, www.reuters.com/article/factcheck-george-floyd-overdose-death/fact-check-no-evidence-drug-overdose-was-main-cause-of-death-for-george-floyd-in-2020-idUSL1N3241XJ/; McKenzie Sadeghi, "Fact check: George Floyd's death ruled a homicide, not fentanyl overdose," *USA Today*, April 26, 2021, www.usatoday.com/story/news/factcheck/2021/04/21/fact-check-george-floyd-autopsy-ruled-his-death-homicide/7317557002/. These are just a few.

7. Number eight in early 2023, according to Similarweb, "Ok.ru," www.similarweb.com/website/ok.ru/#overview/.

8. Shayan Sardarizadeh and Mike Wendling, "Why some people are spreading false rumours about the Texas gunman," BBC News, May 9, 2023, www.bbc.com/news/world-us-canada-65539698/.

9. Social media companies have attempted to adapt after the Christchurch terror attack was livestreamed. Kellen Browning, "Gunman broadcast Buffalo supermarket attack on Twitch," *New York Times*, May 15, 2022, www.nytimes.com/2022/05/14/nyregion/twitch-buffalo-shooting.html/.

10. Office of the New York State Attorney General, "Investigative report on the role of online platforms in the tragic mass shooting in Buffalo on May 14, 2022," October 18, 2022, https://ag.ny.gov/sites/default/files/buffaloshooting-onlineplatformsreport.pdf/.

11. Associated Press, "White racist apologizes for Buffalo market rampage," February 15, 2022, https://newsroom.ap.org/editorial-photos-videos/detail?itemid=90d0518864f54aae851b3bbb53058629&mediatype=video&source=youtube/.

12. Daryl Johnson, "Return of the violent black nationalist," Southern Poverty Law Center, August 8, 2017, www.splcenter.org/fighting-hate/intelligence-report/2017/return-violent-black-nationalist/.

13. Andrew Selsky, Gillian Flaccus and Bernard Condon, "Trump, friends mourn right-wing activist killed in Portland," AP News, May 1, 2021, https://apnews.com/article/ap-top-news-or-state-wire-

politics-shootings-us-news-e86333bf2acf59eb74959af0fee57f9b/. The perpetrator later said in an interview that he was acting in self-defense, but was shot dead in a police raid before his claim was tested in court. Andrew Hay, "Oregon man says Portland shooting was self defense," Reuters, September 3, 2020, www.reuters.com/article/us-global-race-protests-portland/oregon-man-says-portland-shooting-was-self-defense-idUSKBN25U1ND/.

14. Seth G. Jones, Catrina Doxsee and Nicholas Harrington, "The escalating terrorism problem in the United States," November 29, 2022, www.csis.org/analysis/escalating-terrorism-problem-united-states/.

15. Anti-Defamation League, "Murder and extremism in the United States in 2022."

16. Daniel L. Byman, "Assessing the right-wing terror threat in the United States a year after the January 6 insurrection," Brookings, March 9, 2022, www.brookings.edu/blog/order-from-chaos/2022/01/05/assessing-the-right-wing-terror-threat-in-the-united-states-a-year-after-the-january-6-insurrection/.

17. Jacob Ware, "The violent far-right terrorist threat to American law enforcement," Council on Foreign Relations, January 24, 2023, www.cfr.org/blog/violent-far-right-terrorist-threat-american-law-enforcement/.

18. Peter Bergen and David Sterman, "Terrorism in America after 9/11," New America, September 10, 2021, www.newamerica.org/international-security/reports/terrorism-in-america/what-is-the-threat-to-the-united-states-today/.

19. US Department of Homeland Security, "National Terrorism Advisory System bulletin," November 30, 2022, www.dhs.gov/ntas/advisory/national-terrorism-advisory-system-bulletin-november-30-2022/.

20. Federal Bureau of Investigation and Department of Homeland Security, "Strategic intelligence assessment and data on domestic terrorism," May 2021, www.dhs.gov/sites/default/files/publications/21_0514_strategic-intelligence-assessment-data-domestic-terrorism_0.pdf/.

21. US. Government Accountability Office, "The rising threat of domestic terrorism in the U.S. and federal efforts to combat it," March 2, 2023, www.gao.gov/blog/rising-threat-domestic-terrorism-u.s.-and-federal-efforts-combat-it/.

22. Katarzyna Jasko, Gary LaFree, James A. Piazza and Michael Becker, "A comparison of political violence by left-wing, right-wing, and Islamist extremists in the United States and the world," *Proceedings of the National Academy of Sciences of the United States of America* 119, no. 30 (July 18, 2022), https://doi.org/10.1073/pnas.2122593119/; National Consortium for the Study of Terrorism and Responses to Terrorism, "Ideological motivations of terrorism in the United States, 1970–2016," November 2017, www.start.umd.edu/pubs/START_IdeologicalMotivationsOfTerrorismInUS_Nov2017.pdf/.

23. Program on Extremism, "Anarchist/left-wing violent extremism in America: Trends in radicalization, recruitment, and mobilization," November 2021, https://extremism.gwu.edu/sites/g/files/zaxdzs5746/files/Anarchist%20-%20Left-Wing%20Violent%20Extremism%20in%20America.pdf.

24. Committee on Homeland Security, "Subcommittee Chair Bishop: 'It's past time we recognize left-wing violence for what it is,'" May 16, 2023, https://homeland.house.gov/2023/05/16/subcommittee-chair-bishop-its-past-time-we-recognize-left-wing-violence-for-what-it-is/.

25. Philip Bump, "Underrecognized: extremist murders are usually from right-wing actors," *Washington Post*, February 28, 2023, www.washingtonpost.com/politics/2023/02/28/extremism-right-wing-deaths/.

26. Elliot Hannon, "Fox News' Tucker Carlson says white supremacy is a "hoax' and a 'conspiracy theory,'" *Slate Magazine*, August 7, 2019, https://slate.com/news-and-politics/2019/08/fox-news-tucker-carlson-white-supremacy-hoax-conspiracy-theory.html/.

27. Elon Musk (@elonmusk), "Didn't the story come from @ bellingcat, which literally specializes in psychological operations? I don't want to hurt their feelings, but this is either the weirdest story ever or a very bad psyop!", https://twitter.com/elonmusk/status/1655977617583898637/, archived at https://archive.ph/JhQzw/.

28. BBC News, "Alex Jones to pay extra $473m damages over 'fake Sandy Hook' claim," November 10, 2022, www.bbc.com/news/world-us-canada-63592386/.

29. Mike Wendling, "Alex Jones and InfoWars: How Sandy Hook families fought back," BBC News, April 1, 2017, www.bbc.com/news/blogs-trending-39194035/.

30. Kim LaCapria, "ZipRecruiter 'Crisis actors needed in Miami,'" Truth or Fiction?, June 12, 2023, www.truthorfiction.com/ziprecruiter-crisis-actors-needed-in-miami/.

31. Aamer Madhani, "Gun control poll shows mixed results," *USA Today*, December 26, 2012, www.usatoday.com/story/news/nation/2012/12/26/gun-rights-assault-weapons-newtown-shooting/1791827/.

32. Niall McCarthy, "The steady rise of U.S. gun deaths," Statista Daily Data, December 13, 2018, www.statista.com/chart/16421/the-number-of-us-gun-deaths-due-to-firearms/.

33. Nathan Howard, "Driver detained as truck crashes near White House; Nazi flag found," Reuters, May 23, 2023, www.reuters.com/world/us/box-truck-crashes-into-security-barriers-near-white-house-2023-05-23/.

34. *United States v. Kandula*, 1:23-cr-00222, US District Court, District of Columbia, May 23, 2023.

35. Suburban Black Man (@niceblackdude), May 23, 2023, https://twitter.com/roguetrader58/status/1660882362052366336/, archived at https://archive.ph/pKeXB/.

36. Even things that make their opponents look unhinged can be depicted as evidence of the nefarious hand of the deep state. When a man threw himself in front of Donald Trump's motorcade after a court hearing in Miami, a Trump supporter commented, "He must have been a plant." Joshua Chaffin, "How Donald Trump's second arraignment unfolded: Motorcades and MAGA merch in Miami," *Financial Times*, June 14, 2023, www.ft.com/content/1e19569c-9b1d-4c12-a953-4219e371b918/.

37. Elon Musk did not respond to requests for comment.

38. Jasper Ward and Patricia Zengerle, "Gunman kills three, himself in racially motivated shooting," Reuters, August 27, 2023, www.reuters.com/world/us/mayor-number-fatalities-jacksonville-florida-shooting-media-2023-08-26/.

39. "Motive in Nashville shooting remains unclear weeks after 6 people were killed at a Christian school," April 14, 2023, www.nbcnews.

com/news/us-news/motive-nashville-shooting-remains-unclear-weeks-6-people-killed-christ-rcna79700/.

40. Emily West, "The Covenant School parents don't want the shooter's writings released at all. Here's why," News Channel 5 Nashville (WTVF), May 18, 2023, www.newschannel5.com/news/the-covenant-school-parents-dont-want-the-shooters-writings-released-at-all-heres-why/.

41. DC_Draino (@DC_Draino), August 26, 2023, https://twitter.com/DC_Draino/status/1695807896519692599/, archived at https://archive.ph/HCDkO/. DC Draino, real name Rogan O'Handley, did not respond to requests for comment.

42. Travis_in_Flint (@Travis_in_Flint), August 27, 2023, https://twitter.com/Travis_in_Flint/status/1695631412076896293/, archived at https://archive.ph/oeBBP/.

43. Kimberlee Kruesi, "Nashville investigating after possible leak of Covenant shooting images," November 6, 2023, https://apnews.com/article/nashville-covenant-school-shooting-writings-images-49e796dfe610ac9556f9535f4c7d4c72.

44. "Homeland threat assessment," US Department of Homeland Security, October 2020, https://www.dhs.gov/sites/default/files/publications/2020_10_06_homeland-threat-assessment.pdf/.

45. One of the only surviving houses in Lahania was a relatively modest home. Jessica Terrell, "What saved the 'miracle house' in Lahaina?", Honolulu Civil Beat, August 19, 2023, www.civilbeat.org/2023/08/what-saved-the-miracle-house-in-lahaina/.

46. Isaac Stanley-Becker and Shawn Boburg, "Oracle's Larry Ellison joined Nov. 2020 call about contesting Trump's loss," *Washington Post*, May 20, 2022, www.washingtonpost.com/politics/2022/05/20/larry-ellison-oracle-trump-election-challenges/.

47. Shayan Sardarizadeh and Mike Wendling, "Hawaii wildfires: 'Directed energy weapon' and other false claims go viral," BBC News, August 16, 2023, www.bbc.com/news/world-us-canada-66457091/.

48. David E. Sanger and Steven Lee Myers, "China sows disinformation about Hawaii fires using new techniques," *New York Times*, September 11, 2023, www.nytimes.com/2023/09/11/us/politics/china-disinformation-ai.html/.

49. Reem Nadeem, "Inflation, health costs, partisan cooperation among the nation's top problems," Pew Research Center, June 25, 2023,

www.pewresearch.org/politics/2023/06/21/inflation-health-costs-partisan-cooperation-among-the-nations-top-problems/.

50. Josh Crane, "How one QAnon believer escaped the 'Grand Unified Theory Of All Conspiracy Theories,'" WBUR Endless Thread, October 2, 2020, www.wbur.org/endlessthread/2020/10/02/qanon-casualties-conspiracy-theory/.

4 QAnon lives on and on

1. US Justice Department, "Arizona man sentenced to 41 months in prison on felony charge in Jan. 6 Capitol breach," November 17, 2021, www.justice.gov/usao-dc/pr/arizona-man-sentenced-41-months-prison-felony-charge-jan-6-capitol-breach/.

2. Samantha Hawkins, "'QAnon Shaman' will spend over 3 years in prison for Capitol riot," Courthouse News Service, November 17, 2021, www.courthousenews.com/qanon-shaman-will-spend-over-3-years-in-prison-for-capitol-riot/.

3. In July 2023, his legal effort would fail, which for him was probably a positive outcome; if he'd been successful, government prosecutors indicated that they would retry him and ask for a longer sentence. Jordan Fischer, "'Decidedly not exculpatory': Judge denies Jacob Chansley's motion to vacate plea over Jan. 6 footage," WUSA, July 20, 2023, www.wusa9.com/article/news/national/capitol-riots/decidedly-not-exculpatory-judge-denies-jacob-chansleys-motion-to-vacate-plea-over-jan-6-footage-angeli-qanon-shaman-tucker-carlson-fox-news/65-68845a82-7ee1-46b5-bb95-f6663deb5270/.

4. Mike Wendling, "The 'QAnon Shaman' and other Capitol rioters who regret pleading guilty," BBC News, July 15, 2023, www.bbc.com/news/world-us-canada-66169914/.

5. Liz Crokin, "How an STD nearly killed me – and then landed me on welfare," *Marie Claire*, August 16, 2016, www.marieclaire.com/career-advice/a22015/living-on-welfare-herpes/.

6. Will Sommer, "New QAnon-allied GOP Senate candidate also pushed anti-Semitism, flat earthism, and 9/11 conspiracies," *The Daily Beast*, September 16, 2020, www.thedailybeast.com/new-qanon-allied-gop-candidate-lauren-witzke-also-pushed-anti-semitism-flat-earthism-and-911-conspiracies/.

7. Sisco served as Lauren Witzke's campaign manager for a time and had his own political ambitions, running for Congress in a West Virginia House seat in 2022, but pulling out before the primary to back a Trump-endorsed candidate. He became a fan of neo-Nazi Groyper Nick Fuentes and started a blog devoted mainly to Orthodox Christianity and anti-Semitic themes. When I spoke to him in 2023, he said he stuck by his monarchist political ideas, but was giving "mainstream politics" a break. Lauren Witzke herself, despite her assistance at the event in Scranton and her help in later organizing our interview with Stew Peters, did not respond to my requests for further comment.

8. Elizabeth Cassin and Mike Wendling, "QAnon: What's the truth behind a pro-Trump conspiracy theory?", BBC News, August 2, 2018, www.bbc.com/news/blogs-trending-45040614/.

9. Mack Lamoureux, "Q is dead, long live QAnon," *Vice News*, November 15, 2022, www.vice.com/en/article/wxnkzq/qanon-q-drop-midterms/.

10. Brigham Tomco, "Attorney for former OUR employees says they 'affirm' allegations of sexual misconduct against Tim Ballard," *Deseret News*, September 29, 2023, www.deseret.com/utah/2023/9/28/23894444/operation-underground-railroad-tim-ballard-allegations/.

11. Kevin Roose, "QAnon followers are hijacking the #SaveTheChildren movement," *New York Times*, August 12, 2020, www.nytimes.com/2020/08/12/technology/qanon-save-the-children-trafficking.html/.

12. Adrenochrome is a real substance, but as a chemical is rather banal; the idea that it gives eternal life or an awesome high was apparently invented by Hunter S. Thompson. Jordan Hoffman, "Jim Caviezel decries 'the adrenochroming of children,' as if that's a thing," *Vanity Fair*, April 17, 2021, www.vanityfair.com/hollywood/2021/04/jim-caviezel-decries-the-adrenochroming-of-children-as-if-thats-a-thing/.

13. Anders Anglesey, "Jim Caviezel emulates 'Braveheart' speech to cheering crowd at QAnon convention," *Newsweek*, October 25, 2021, www.newsweek.com/jim-caviezel-braveheart-qanon-convention-las-vegas-1642133/.

5   Proud Boys and "groomers"

1.   Harriet Alexander, "Proud Boys chairman and Trump supporter stabbed in brawl close to White House," *The Independent*, November 4, 2020, www.independent.co.uk/news/world/americas/us-election-2020/proud-boys-stabbed-washington-dc-enrique-tarrio-bevelyn-beatty-b1595242.html/.

2.   Emily Zantow, "'Don't leave': Tarrio's orders for Jan. 6 riot on display," Courthouse News Service, January 30, 2023, www.courthousenews.com/dont-leave-tarrios-orders-for-jan-6-riot-on-display/.

3.   Matt Lavietes, "Protesters are bloodied and arrested at NYC Drag Story Hour," NBC News, March 20, 2023, www.nbcnews.com/nbc-out/out-news/protesters-bloodied-arrested-nyc-drag-story-hour-rcna75724/.

4.   You can see pictures of the sign and T-shirt, which hinted at pedophilia rumors about President Biden at: Dean Moses, "'Hate has no home in New York': Chaos ensues at West Village Drag Story Hour Read-A-Thon," amNew York, March 19, 2023, www.amny.com/news/chaos-west-village-drag-story-hour-read-a-thon/.

5.   Kyle Schnitzer and Jorge Fitz-Gibbon, "AG Letitia James' 'Drag Story Hour' draws over 100 supporters, protesters, cops, even NYC Council guards," *New York Post*, March 20, 2023, https://nypost.com/2023/03/19/nyc-drag-story-hour-draws-protesters-cops-even-city-council-guards/.

6.   Nick Gass, "Trump: Transgender people can use whatever bathroom they want," *Politico*, April 21, 2016, www.politico.com/blogs/2016-gop-primary-live-updates-and-results/2016/04/trump-transgender-bathrooms-222257/.

7.   Anne D. Innocenzio, "Target becomes latest company to suffer backlash for LGBTQ+ support, pulls some Pride month clothing," Associated Press, May 25, 2023, https://apnews.com/article/target-pride-lgbtq-4bc9de6339f86748bcb8a453d7b9acf0/.

8.   Institute of Strategic Dialogue, "Anti-drag mobilization efforts targeting LGBTQ+ people in the US," June 30, 2023, www.isdglobal.org/isd-publications/a-year-of-hate-anti-drag-mobilization-efforts-targeting-lgbtq-people-in-the-us/.

9.   In the end, although it stuck in my mind, our interview with Dixon didn't quite fit our half-hour film, and the footage we shot with her

did not make the final cut. "Portland's battleground," BBC World News, March 9, 2019, www.bbc.co.uk/programmes/b0c6f888/.

10. Joseph Bernstein, "Andy Ngo has the newest new media career. It's made him a victim and a star," BuzzFeed News, July 19, 2019, www.buzzfeednews.com/article/josephbernstein/andy-ngo-portland-antifa/.

11. United States Holocaust Memorial Museum, "Degenerate Art," https://encyclopedia.ushmm.org/content/en/article/degenerate-art-1/.

12. Mike Wendling, "Ray Epps: Target of Capitol riot conspiracy theories charged over January 6," BBC News, September 20, 2023, www.bbc.com/news/world-us-canada-66860910/.

13. Tyler Kingkade, "'We're Coming For Your Children' chant at NYC Drag March elicits outrage, but activists say it's taken out of context," NBC News, June 27, 2023, www.nbcnews.com/nbc-out/nbc-out-proud/re-coming-children-chant-nyc-drag-march-elicits-outrage-activists-say-rcna91341/.

14. DC_Draino (@DC_Draino), "Leftist Radicals: 'Stop calling us groomers & pedos – we are not coming for your children'. Also Leftist Radicals: 'We're here, we're queer, we're coming for your children.'" June 26, 2023, https://twitter.com/DC_Draino/status/1673355631791620097/, archived at https://archive.ph/FzPjY/.

15. Melissa Goldin, "Changes to Connecticut's anti-discrimination laws won't make pedophiles a protected class," Associated Press, May 26, 2023, https://apnews.com/article/fact-check-connecticut-bill-pedophiles-005592794463/.

16. David Strom, "Connecticut follows Minnesota in first step to normalize pedophilia," Hotair, May 17, 2023, https://hotair.com/david-strom/2023/05/17/connecticut-follows-minnesota-in-first-step-to-normalize-pedophilia-n551347/.

17. Tucker Carlson (@TuckerCarlson), "Ep. 2 Cling to your taboos!" https://twitter.com/TuckerCarlson/status/16669 28190445477890/, archived at https://archive.ph/Lw4jM/.

18. For starters: James Vincent, "Instagram's recommendation algorithms are promoting pedophile networks," The Verge, June 7, 2023, www.theverge.com/2023/6/7/23752192/instagrams-recommendation-algorithms-promote-pedophile-networks-

investigation/; Todd Spangler, "Instagram algorithms connect 'vast' network of pedophiles seeking child pornography, according to researchers," *Variety*, June 7, 2023, https://variety.com/2023/digital/news/instagram-pedophile-network-child-pornography-researchers-1235635743/; Natasha Lomas "Meta warned it faces 'heavy sanctions' in EU if it fails to fix child protection issues on Instagram," June 8, 2023, https://techcrunch.com/2023/06/08/meta-child-protection-dsa-warning/. There were many others, including stories in *The Guardian*, *Independent*, Fox News, *Daily Mail*, *Politico* and others.

19. Tucker Carlson did not respond to requests for comment.

6   *Anti-vaccine derangement syndrome*

1. Jennifer Korn and Oliver Darcy, "'Monday Night Football' telecast in which Hamlin collapsed was most watched in ESPN's history," CNN, January 4, 2023, www.cnn.com/2023/01/04/media/monday-night-football-ratings-espn-damar-hamlin/index.html/.

2. Emerald Robinson (@EmeraldRobinson), January 3, 2023, https://twitter.com/EmeraldRobinson/status/1610270781724065794/, archived at https://archive.ph/X2jm0/.

3. Charlie Kirk (@charliekirk11), January 2, 2023, https://twitter.com/charliekirk11/status/1610106783519092741/. Archived at https://archive.ph/eormR/.

4. Died Suddenly (@DiedSuddenly_), https://twitter.com/DiedSuddenly_/status/1610103839910158344/, archived at https://archive.ph/cSC2Q/.

5. Miguel Gallegos, Viviane De Castro Pecanha and Tomás Caycho-Rodríguez. "Anti-vax: The history of a scientific problem," *Journal of Public Health* 45, no. 1 (April 16, 2022): e140–41. https://doi.org/10.1093/pubmed/fdac048/.

6. Kaleigh Rogers, "Republicans aren't new to the anti-vaxx movement," FiveThirtyEight, September 9, 2021, https://fivethirtyeight.com/features/republicans-arent-new-to-the-anti-vaxx-movement/.

7. "Cumulative confirmed COVID-19 deaths by world region," Our World in Data, https://ourworldindata.org/grapher/cumulative-covid-deaths-region/.

8. Daniel Funke, "Fact-checking 'Plandemic': A documentary full of false conspiracy theories about the coronavirus," Politifact, May 7, 2020, www.politifact.com/article/2020/may/08/fact-checking-plandemic-documentary-full-false-con/.

9. Kristen V. Brown, "Meet the man behind the modern anti-vaccine movement," Bloomberg, March 23, 2021. www.bloomberg.com/news/articles/2021-03-23/meet-the-man-behind-the-modern-anti-vaccine-movement/.

10. UK Government, "Childhood vaccines: Parental attitudes survey 2022 findings," February 20, 2023. www.gov.uk/government/publications/childhood-vaccines-parental-attitudes-survey-2022/childhood-vaccines-parental-attitudes-survey-2022-findings/.

11. Jan Hoffman, "President Trump on vaccines: From skeptic to cheerleader," *New York Times*, March 11, 2020, www.nytimes.com/2020/03/09/health/trump-vaccines.html/.

12. Jon Cohen, "Unveiling 'Warp Speed,' the White House's America-first push for a coronavirus vaccine," *Science*, May 12, 2020, www.science.org/content/article/unveiling-warp-speed-white-house-s-america-first-push-coronavirus-vaccine/.

13. Allan Smith, "Trump booed at Alabama rally after telling supporters to get vaccinated," CNBC, August 23, 2021, www.cnbc.com/2021/08/22/trump-booed-at-alabama-rally-after-telling-supporters-to-get-vaccinated.html/; Jill Colvin, "Trump reveals he got COVID-19 booster shot; crowd boos him," Associated Press, December 20, 2021, https://apnews.com/article/coronavirus-pandemic-health-donald-trump-coronavirus-vaccine-74abcd4e6833835f5df445fe2142e22b/.

14. Editorial Board, "Trump's effort to disavow Operation Warp Speed shows how far he's fallen," *New York Post*, February 6, 2023, https://nypost.com/2023/02/05/trumps-effort-to-disavow-operation-warp-speed-shows-how-far-hes-fallen/.

15. Brett Samuels, "Trump won't say if COVID vaccines work: 'Not a great thing to talk about' as a Republican," *The Hill*, June 21, 2023, https://thehill.com/homenews/4059468-trump-wont-say-if-covid-vaccines-work-not-a-great-thing-to-talk-about-as-a-republican/.

16. Stew Peters (@RealStewPeters), "This is how you treat the FAKE MSM. BBC doesn't want you to see this. WATCH FULL

INTERVIEW [Link]," May 4, 2023, https://twitter.com/realstewpeters/status/1653957954024898560/, archived at https://archive.ph/nCkNW/.

7   No political solution

1. Joelle Jones, "'Love will always win': Oregon City hosts Pride Night," KOIN, June 24, 2023, www.koin.com/local/clackamas-county/oregon-city-pride-event-06242023/.

2. Zane Sparling, "2 arrested during brawl between Proud Boys, nationalists protesting Oregon City Pride, police and witness say," Oregon Live, June 28, 2023, www.oregonlive.com/crime/2023/06/2-arrested-during-brawl-between-proud-boys-nationalists-protesting-oregon-city-pride-police-and-witness-say.html/.

3. Gavin McInnes (@RealGavinMcInnes), "Masked Feds show up to Proud Boys event. PBs immediately call them out, tune them up, and demask them. #POYFB #FAFO," June 25, 2023, https://t.me/RealGavinMcInnes/3194/, archived at https://archive.ph/WsP6R/.

4. Gavin McInnes (@RealGavinMcInnes), "I'm told this is one of the Patriot Front Feds the Proud Boys unmasked. He is Jewish and says he plans to work for the gov't after he graduates. Huge if true," June 25, 2023, https://t.me/RealGavinMcInnes/3195/, archived at https://archive.ph/Y5dsb/.

5. Elon Musk (@elonmusk), https://twitter.com/elonmusk/status/1673683343169159168/, June 27, 2023, archived at https://archive.ph/talit/.

6. Associated Press, "Elon Musk facing defamation lawsuit in Texas over posts that falsely identified man in protest," October 2, 2023, https://apnews.com/article/elon-musk-defamation-lawsuit-proud-boys-texas-f353a740a9e6af6b5d6672b9d7f0ed2c/.

7. Arizona Proud Boys (@ArizonaProudBoys), "It's easy to understand why small groups like 'Patriot Front' (around 200 members nationwide) and the 'Active Club' (around 88 members nationwide) are trying to recruit off of our success and showing up to our events ...," June 27, 2023, https://t.me/ArizonaProudBoys/198/, archived at https://archive.ph/nCkNW/.

8. Some researchers call it an ideology more than an organization. "Three Percenters," Southern Poverty Law Center, www.splcenter. org/fighting-hate/extremist-files/group/three-percenters/.

9. The Three Percenters Organization, "TTPO's final statement," February 21, 2021, archived at https://web.archive.org/ web/20210310130503/https://thethreepercenters.org/2021/02/ ttpos-final-statement/21/.

10. Mike Wendling, "Stewart Rhodes' son: 'How I escaped my father's militia,'" BBC News, November 29, 2022, www.bbc.com/news/ world-us-canada-63709446/.

11. Martha Bellisle, "31 Patriot Front members arrested near Idaho pride event," Associated Press, June 12, 2022, https://apnews.com/ article/coeur-dalene-idaho-government-and-politics-arrests-01fd1 5f6d3b3bcab9404106c85f673c3/.

12. Ibid.

13. Patriot Front, https://bloodandsoil.org/.

14. Patriot Front, "Life Liberty Victory," https://patriotfront.us/ manifesto/.

15. Sergio Olmos, "'We are desperate for new people': Inside a hate group's leaked online chats," The Guardian, February 8, 2022, www.theguardian.com/world/2022/jan/28/leaked-online-chats-white-nationalist-patriot-front/.

16. Anti-Defamation League, "White supremacist propaganda soars to all-time high in 2022," March 8, 2023, www.adl.org/resources/ report/white-supremacist-propaganda-soars-all-time-high-2022.

17. Gabe Gutierrez, "Ron DeSantis signs legislation to combat hate crimes while on trip to Israel," NBC News, April 27, 2023, www.nbcnews.com/politics/2024-election/ron-desantis-signs-bill-combat-hate-crimes-israel-rcna81799/.

18. Maya Pottiger, "Far-right group Patriot Front marched down the Mall on Saturday night," Washingtonian, December 6, 2021, www. washingtonian.com/2021/12/06/far-right-group-patriot-front-marched-down-the-mall-on-saturday-night/.

19. Evan Koslof, "Meet the man who went viral heckling white supremacists protesting on the National Mall," WUSA, May 17, 2023, www.wusa9.com/article/news/politics/bike-riding-patriot-front-heckler-joe-flood-goes-viral-national-mall-white-supremacist-protest/65-30aff9b5-d8ba-48a8-91b7-fdd463855250/.

20. "Wall Street Silver" (@WallStreetSilv), https://twitter.com/WallStreetSilv/status/1657479699101102083/, archived at https://archive.ph/qg7wy/.

21. Jonathan Lewis, Joshua Molloy and Graham Macklin, "The lineage of violence: Saints culture and militant accelerationist terrorism," Global Network on Extremism and Technology, April 27, 2023, https://gnet-research.org/2023/04/27/the-lineage-of-violence-saints-culture-and-militant-accelerationist-terrorism/.

22. Mike Wendling, "How the US power grid is a target for far-right groups," BBC News, March 10, 2023, www.bbc.com/news/world-us-canada-64832129/.

23. Ilana Krill and Bennett Clifford, "Report: Mayhem, murder, and misdirection: Violent extremist attack plots against critical infrastructure in the United States, 2016–2022," George Washington University Program on Extremism, September 2022, https://extremism.gwu.edu/report-mayhem-murder-and-misdirection-violent-extremist-attack-plots-against-critical-infrastructure/.

24. Lukáš Diko, Karin Kovary Solymos, Aktuality.sk, Ali Winston and Martin Laine, "Bratislava terrorist radicalized on Terrorgram, its members take credit," VSquare, November 9, 2022, https://vsquare.org/bratislava-terrorist-radicalized-on-terrorgram-its-members-take-credit/.

8 Christian nationalists and radical moms

1. I was tipped off about The Hollow by a local activist, Carol Lerner.

2. Jeffrey M. Jones, "How Religious Are Americans?", Gallup, May 31, 2023, https://news.gallup.com/poll/358364/religious-americans.aspx/.

3. Reem Nadeem, "Views of the U.S. as a 'Christian nation' and opinions about 'Christian nationalism,'" Pew Research Center, November 23, 2022, www.pewresearch.org/religion/2022/10/27/views-of-the-u-s-as-a-christian-nation-and-opinions-about-christian-nationalism/.

4. David Klepper, "Trump arrest prompts Jesus comparisons: 'Spiritual warfare,'" Associated Press, April 5, 2023, https://apnews.com/article/donald-trump-arraignment-jesus-christ-conspiracy-theory-670c45bd71b3466dcd6e8e188badcd1d.

5. Michelle R. Smith and Richard Lardner, "Michael Flynn is recruiting an 'Army of God' in growing Christian nationalist movement," Associated Press/PBS NewsHour, October 7, 2022, www.pbs.org/newshour/politics/michael-flynn-is-recruiting-an-army-of-god-in-growing-christian-nationalist-movement/.

6. Ibid.

7. Alex Morris, "Michael Flynn and the Christian right's plan to turn America into a theocracy," *Rolling Stone*, November 21, 2021, www.rollingstone.com/politics/politics-features/michael-flynn-cornerstone-church-christian-theocracy-1260606/.

8. Michael Flynn did not respond to requests for comment.

9. Kara Voght, "The MAGAmerican dream lives in Sarasota," *Washington Post*, October 4, 2023, www.washingtonpost.com/style/power/interactive/2023/sarasota-maga-dream/.

10. Hollow 2A, "General Flynn | Moms of America," February 23, 2022, https://rumble.com/vvnuxe-general-flynn-moms-of-america-the-hollow-2a-venice.html/.

11. Martin Pengelly, "Illinois Republican Mary Miller sorry for quoting Hitler in Capitol speech," *The Guardian*, January 11, 2021, www.theguardian.com/us-news/2021/jan/10/illinois-republican-mary-miller-hitler-capitol-speech/.

12. Moms for America, "2021: Year in review," https://momsforamerica.us/wp-content/uploads/2022/02/2021-Year-In-Review-Moms-For-America.pdf/, archived at https://archive.ph/32JKx/.

13. Olivia Little, "Moms for Liberty members have been linked to incidents of harassment and threats around the country," Media Matters for America, April 11, 2023, www.mediamatters.org/moms-liberty/moms-liberty-members-have-been-linked-incidents-harassment-and-threats-around-country/.

14. MSNBC, "Field Report with Paola Ramos," August 7, 2022, https://archive.org/details/MSNBCW_20220808_030000_Field_Report_With_Paola_Ramos/start/660/end/720/.

15. Kiera Butler, "My Deeply unsettling return to the Moms for Liberty conference," *Mother Jones*, July 2023, www.motherjones.com/politics/2023/07/moms-for-liberty-conference/; Bianca Seward and Gabe Gutierrez, "'Never apologize': How Moms for Liberty teaches its members to spin the media," NBC, July 2, 2023, www.

nbcnews.com/politics/2024-election/moms-liberty-teaching-members-spin-media-rcna92099/.

16. Video archived at www.mediamatters.org/media/4008037/.

17. Ziegler and her husband Christian Ziegler, who in 2023 was voted chairman of the Florida Republican Party, were once the golden couple of conservative politics in the state, until later that year when Mr. Ziegler was accused of raping a woman who had previously had a sexual encounter with the couple. Commentators noted the irony of the family-values, anti-LGBTQ pair being involved in kinky sex and, in Mr. Ziegler's case, possibly even sexual assault.

18. Earle Kimel, "'Baby Killer': Attack message on mobile billboard shows rancor in Sarasota School Board races," *Sarasota Herald-Tribune*, August 12, 2022, www.heraldtribune.com/story/news/education/2022/08/12/sarasota-school-board-election-mobile-billboard-underscores-rancor-race/10273313002/.

19. David Gilbert, "MAGA School Board candidates celebrated victory with Proud Boys flashing white power signs," Vice News, August 26, 2022, www.vice.com/en/article/7k8k7y/sarasota-school-board-proud-boys/.

20. Brooke Schultz and Geoff Mulvihill, "Liberal and moderate candidates take control of school boards in contentious races across US," Associated Press, November 8, 2023, https://apnews.com/article/school-board-elections-moms-liberty-progressives-1e439de49b0e8498537484fb031f66a6/.

21. Selene San Felice and Sara Fischer, "With Trump and Rumble, Florida becomes conservative media HQ," Axios, April 26, 2022, www.axios.com/local/tampa-bay/2022/04/26/florida-conservative-media-hq-trump-rumble/.

22. "Trump says he'll bring back Michael Flynn if he's re-elected," MSNBC, May 15, 2023, www.youtube.com/watch?v=J3CAasx8Uqo/, archived at https://archive.ph/wip/DDHVK/.

9   *The perpetual influencer machine*

1. There was, of course, no Covid lockdown later in 2023.

2. Mike Wendling, "Bankrupt Alex Jones spends nearly $100,000 a month," BBC News, February 16, 2023, www.bbc.com/news/

world-us-canada-64644080/. Alex Jones did not respond to requests for comment.

3. For instance: Nate Cohn, "The new Republican establishment," *New York Times*, October 12, 2023, www.nytimes.com/2023/10/12/upshot/new-republican-establishment-speaker.html/; Stephen Collinson, "New CNN poll shows Trump is in a league of his own as GOP primary hits fall sprint," CNN, September 5, 2023, www.cnn.com/2023/09/05/politics/trump-gop-primary-2024/index.html/. Benjamin Wallace-Wells, "Is Trump just an ordinary Republican now?", *The New Yorker*, September 25, 2023, www.newyorker.com/news/the-political-scene/is-trump-just-an-ordinary-republican-now/; Elvia Díaz, "Matt Salmon's Steve Bannon tweet proves one thing: It's Trump's Republican Party now," Arizona Republic, October 25, 2021, https://www.azcentral.com/story/opinion/op-ed/elviadiaz/2021/10/25/matt-salmon-tweet-proves-trump-republican-party-now/8544658002/.

4. Mike Wendling, "Robert F Kennedy Jr is running for president as an independent. Who will vote for him?", BBC News, October 9, 2023, www.bbc.com/news/world-us-canada-67035600/.

5. Walter Isaacson, "The real story of Musk's Twitter takeover," *Wall Street Journal*, August 31, 2023, www.wsj.com/tech/elon-musk-twitter-x-takeover-walter-isaacson-5f553fa/.

6. Mike Wendling and Will Yates, "Gab: Free speech haven or alt-right safe space?", BBC News, December 14, 2016, www.bbc.com/news/blogs-trending-38305402/.

7. Anti-Defamation League, "Tree of Life shooting revives 'optics' debate among white supremacists," February 21, 2023, www.adl.org/resources/blog/tree-life-shooting-revives-optics-debate-among-white-supremacists/.

8. WPXI, "Gab CEO testifies about Bowers' social media posts during Pittsburgh Synagogue shooting trial," June 12, 2023, www.yahoo.com/lifestyle/pittsburgh-synagogue-shooting-trial-day-121212681.html/.

9. Jeff Horwitz and Keach Hagey, "Parler makes play for conservatives mad at Facebook, Twitter," *Wall Street Journal*, November 15, 2020, www.wsj.com/articles/parler-backed-by-mercer-family-makes-play-for-conservatives-mad-at-facebook-twitter-11605382430/.

10. Reuters, "Conglomerate Starboard buys Parler, to shut down social media app temporarily," April 14, 2023, www.reuters.com/markets/deals/parler-shut-down-temporarily-after-starboard-buys-social-media-platform-2023-04-14/.

11. *US Dominion, Inc. v. Fox News Network, LLC*, Superior Court of Delaware, December 16, 2021, CA. N21C-03-257 EMD.

12. Stephen Bannon did not respond to requests for comment.

13. Revolver News, "Meet Ray Epps: The fed-protected provocateur who appears to have led the very first 1/6 attack on the US Capitol," October 25, 2021, www.revolver.news/2021/10/meet-ray-epps-the-fed-protected-provocateur-who-appears-to-have-led-the-very-first-1-6-attack-on-the-u-s-capitol/.

14. David Giuliani, "Fuentes victim of 'swatting' incidents: Cops," La Grange, Patch, January 6, 2023, https://patch.com/illinois/lagrange/fuentes-victim-swatting-incidents-cops/.

15. Through a representative, Joe Rogan declined a request for an interview.

16. Zack Beauchamp, "Bernie Sanders's Joe Rogan experience," *Vox*, January 24, 2020, www.vox.com/policy-and-politics/2020/1/24/21080234/bernie-sanders-joe-rogan-experience-endorsement-controversy/.

17. Media Matters for America, "Joe Rogan says conspiracy theorist 'Alex Jones was right about a lot of stuff,'" September 30, 2020, www.mediamatters.org/joe-rogan-experience/joe-rogan-says-conspiracy-theorist-alex-jones-was-right-about-lot-stuff/.

18. Mark Leibovich, "Being Glenn Beck," *New York Times*, September 29, 2010, www.nytimes.com/2010/10/03/magazine/03beck-t.html/.

19. Nicholas Schmidle, "Glenn Beck tries out decency," *The New Yorker*, November 7, 2016, www.newyorker.com/magazine/2016/11/14/glenn-beck-tries-out-decency/.

20. Jones' book was subtitled "And the War for the World"; Beck's was more specific: "Joe Biden and the Rise of Twenty-First-Century Fascism."

21. BBC Trending, "What is the Great Reset – and how did it get hijacked by conspiracy theories?", June 23, 2021, www.bbc.com/news/blogs-trending-57532368/. Both men got praised by influential conservative group Turning Point USA: Alex Griffing,

"Alex Jones gets standing ovation from TPUSA crowd when introduced by Charlie Kirk," Mediaite, September 19, 2022, www.mediaite.com/news/alex-jones-gets-standing-ovation-by-tpusa-crowd-when-introduced-by-charlie-kirk/.

22. Glenn Beck did not respond to requests for comment.

23. Byrn Nelson, "How stochastic terrorism uses disgust to incite violence," *Scientific American*, November 5, 2022, www.scientificamerican.com/article/how-stochastic-terrorism-uses-disgust-to-incite-violence/.

24. Mike Wendling, "Wadea al-Fayoume: Last words of knifed US Muslim boy were 'Mom, I'm fine,'" BBC News, October 16, 2023, www.bbc.com/news/world-us-canada-67085553.

25. Reuters, "Former Hamas chief calls for protests, neighbours to join war against Israel," October 11, 2023, www.reuters.com/world/middle-east/former-hamas-chief-calls-protests-neighbours-join-war-against-israel-2023-10-11/.

26. David Gilbert, "Rumors of a 'Global Day of Jihad' have unleashed a dangerous wave of disinformation," *Wired*, October 13, 2023, www.wired.com/story/day-of-jihad-disinformation-israel-palestine/.

27. The case was due to go to trial in January 2024. Mike Wendling, "Man pleads not guilty to murder of US Muslim boy," BBC News, October 30, 2023, www.bbc.com/news/world-us-canada-67267319/.

10 Revenge of the normies

1. Christopher Harress and Galen Bacharie, "Auditor pick spurs fury, push for election: Interim choice linked to online conspiracy posts," *Des Moines Register*, June 20, 2023, www.desmoinesregister.com/story/news/politics/2023/06/20/auditor-appointment-in-iowa-spurs-fury-scramble-for-special-election/70314434007/.

2. Ibid. Mark Snell did not respond to requests for comment.

3. Sheera Frenkel, "Proud Boys regroup, focusing on school boards and town councils," *New York Times*, December 14, 2021, www.nytimes.com/2021/12/14/us/proud-boys-local-issues.html/.

4. Zac Anderson, "Proud Boy says his group 'greatly involved' in Sarasota School Board campaigns," *Sarasota Herald-Tribune*, September 2, 2022, https://eu.heraldtribune.com/story/news/

politics/2022/09/02/extremist-group-played-big-role-school-campaigns-members-says/7971147001/.

5. Ari Berman, "New report: One-third of states have an election denier overseeing elections," *Mother Jones*, September 17, 2023, www.motherjones.com/politics/2023/09/one-third-states-election-denier-governor-attorney-general-secretary/.

6. Jim Marchant did not respond to requests for comment, nor did Wayne Willott, the man who goes by the alias "Juan O Savin."

7. It appears from Savin's own statements that "107" is a roundabout reference to the number 17, which corresponds to the letter Q and is feted by QAnon fans. Bill McCarthy, "A coalition of 'stop the steal' Republicans aims to take control of elections. QAnon is helping," Poynter, June 8, 2022, www.poynter.org/fact-checking/2022/juan-o-savin-stop-the-steal-republicans-control-elections-qanon/.

8. Mike Wendling and Shayan Sardarizadeh, "US midterms: The election deniers running to control 2024 vote," BBC News, November 3, 2022, www.bbc.co.uk/news/world-us-canada-63490938/.

9. "America First SOS Coalition," https://americafirstsos.com/.

10. Lake was running for governor, while her fellow Republican Mark Finchem ran for Arizona Secretary of State, hoping for an election denial one-two punch in a state that has increasingly become a center for election conspiracies.

11. For some insightful analysis on this, see Isabel Jones, Lucy Cooper, Sabine Lawrence, Rhea Bhatnagar, Eric Levai, Ciaran O'Connor and Jared Holt, "Five key takeaways from election denialist activity during the 2022 midterms," Institute of Strategic Dialogue, April 17, 2023, www.isdglobal.org/digital_dispatches/election-denialist-trends-us-midterms-retrospective/.

12. Melanie Zanona and Annie Grayer, "'Not what it was': House Freedom Caucus wrestles with its future amid split over tactics and Trump," CNN, July 10, 2023, https://edition.cnn.com/2023/07/10/politics/house-freedom-caucus-future-plans/index.html/.

13. For instance, fellow Freedom Caucus member the QAnon-amplifying Lauren Boebert (@laurenboebert) on Capitol rioters: "They're drug-testing Brandon for protesting at the Capitol but won't drug test the folks in the White House where cocaine was just found!" July 14, 2023, https://twitter.com/laurenboebert/

status/1679980061733146625/, archived at https://archive.ph/zNeCo/; on pedophilia, a clip of Joe Biden joking around with a small child: "This is not normal behavior for a President with a child that he doesn't even know. How long are they going to continue to let him do this stuff?", July 14, 2023, https://twitter.com/laurenboebert/status/1679927100382515201/, archived at https://archive.ph/Pq9MN/.

14. Christopher Mathias (@letsgomathias), "Here's the back of Tiny's shirt, which makes the meaning clear. (This shirt was everywhere at rallies from 2017-2020.)," May 7, 2023, https://twitter.com/letsgomathias/status/1655342552264974337/, archived at https://archive.ph/WJMRE/.

15. April Ehrlich, "Proud Boy Tusitala 'Tiny' Toese sentenced to 8 years for violence at Portland rallies," Oregon Public Broadcasting, July 21, 2023, www.opb.org/article/2023/07/21/proud-boy-tusitala-tiny-toese-sentenced-8-years-prison-violence-portland-rallies/.

16. BBC World Service, "The Documentary: America's own extremists," June 28, 2011, www.bbc.co.uk/programmes/poohffbp/.

Conclusion: Day of reckoning

1. Christopher Weber and Richard Vogel, "California shop owner killed over Pride flag was adamant she would never take it down, friend says," AP News, August 23, 2023, https://apnews.com/article/pride-flag-store-shooting-california-b2bd4f89e992356f35d2101cdf665acb/.

2. Eric Bonetto and Thomas Arciszewski, "The creativity of conspiracy theories," *Journal of Creative Behavior* 55, no. 4 (March 25, 2021): 916–24, https://doi.org/10.1002/jocb.497/.

3. Tucker Carlson (@TuckerCarlson), https://x.com/TuckerCarlson/status/1694513603251241143/, archived at https://archive.ph/mLBYE. Within 24 hours, the tweet had been seen, according to X/Twitter's metrics, more than 230 million times, although the actual number of video views was lower, and the company counts any view for two seconds or longer.

4. Andrew Zhang, "Ramaswamy faces scrutiny over suggesting government involvement in 9/11," Politico, August 22, 2023, www.

politico.com/news/2023/08/22/ramaswamy-scrutiny-9-11-00112302/.

5. FiveThirtyEight, "Latest polls," October 13, 2023, https://projects.fivethirtyeight.com/polls/president-primary-r/2024/national/.

6. Mike Wendling, "Robert F Kennedy Jr is running for president as an independent. Who will vote for him?", BBC News, October 9, 2023, www.bbc.co.uk/news/world-us-canada-67035600.

7. Republican National Committee, "RNC launches 'Bank Your Vote' campaign," June 7, 2023, https://gop.com/press-release/rnc-launches-bank-your-vote-campaign/, archived at https://archive.ph/M1ldX/.

8. Wallace Jacob, Paul Goldsmith-Pinkham and Jason L. Schwartz, "Excess death rates for Republican and Democratic registered voters in Florida and Ohio during the COVID-19 pandemic," *JAMA Internal Medicine*, July 24, 2023, https://doi.org/10.1001/jamainternmed.2023.1154/.

9. J. Miles Coleman and Kyle Kondik, "A brief history of electoral college bias," Center for Politics, July 6, 2023, https://centerforpolitics.org/crystalball/articles/a-brief-history-of-electoral-college-bias/.

10. Public Religion Research Institute, "Threats to American democracy ahead of an unprecedented presidential election," October 25, 2023, www.prri.org/research/threats-to-american-democracy-ahead-of-an-unprecedented-presidential-election/.

11. BBC News, "Trump presidency: Protests turn violent in Portland, Oregon," November 11, 2016, www.bbc.com/news/election-us-2016-37946231/.

12. Associated Press, "Trump tells 'Meet the Press' he might pardon Enrique Tarrio, other Jan. 6 rioters," September 18, 2023, www.al.com/news/2023/09/trump-tells-meet-the-press-he-might-pardon-enrique-tarrio-other-jan-6-rioters.html/.

13. Anthony Zurcher, "What a Donald Trump second term would look like," BBC News, November 3, 2023, www.bbc.co.uk/news/world-us-canada-67272569.

14. Associated Press, "At statehouses across US, hundreds rally in support of Trump," January 6, 2021, www.csmonitor.com/USA/Politics/2021/0106/At-statehouses-across-US-hundreds-rally-in-support-of-Trump/.

15. Elizabeth Williamson, "How a small town silenced a neo-nazi hate campaign," *New York Times*, June 22, 2023, www.nytimes.

com/2021/09/05/us/politics/nazi-whitefish-charlottesville.
html/.

16. Ellen Wexler, "After the cyber storm," *Moment Magazine*, September 14, 2021, https://momentmag.com/report-from-whitefish/.

Further reading

In addition to the sources cited in the endnotes, the following books were among the titles I found most helpful in my reporting and work to understand recent American political developments.

A Lot of People Are Saying: The New Conspiracism and the Assault on Democracy by Nancy L. Rosenblum and Russell Muirhead, 2019.

American Psychosis: A Historical Investigation of How the Republican Party Went Crazy by David Corn, 2022.

Anti-Social: Online Extremists, Techno-Utopians and the Hijacking of the American Conversation by Andrew Marantz, 2019.

Blowback: A Warning to Save Democracy from the Next Trump by Miles Taylor, 2023.

Bring the War Home: The White Power Movement and Paramilitary America by Kathleen Belew, 2018.

Conspiracy Theories and the People Who Believe Them edited by Joseph E. Uscinski, 2018.

Doppelganger: A Trip into the Mirror World by Naomi Klein, 2023.

Everything You Love Will Burn: Inside the Rebirth of White Nationalism in America by Vegas Tenold, 2018.

Extremism by J. M. Berger, 2018.

Far-Right Vanguard: The Radical Roots of Modern Conservatism by John S. Huntington, 2021.

Going Mainstream: How Extremists are Taking Over by Julia Ebner, 2023.

Hate in the Homeland: The New Global Far Right by Cynthia Miller-Idriss, 2020.

How Civil Wars Start: And How to Stop Them by Barbara F. Walter, 2022.

Meme Wars: The Untold Story of the Online Battles Upending Democracy in America by Joan Donovan, Emily Dreyfuss and Brian Friedberg, 2022.

Off the Edge: Flat Earthers, Conspiracy Culture and Why People Will Believe Anything by Kelly Weill, 2022.

On Disinformation: How to Fight Truth and Protect Democracy by Lee McIntyre, 2023.

Pastels and Pedophiles: Inside the Mind of QAnon by Mia Bloom and Sophia Moskalenko, 2021.

People Love Dead Jews: Reports from a Haunted Present by Dara Horn, 2021.

Red Pill, Blue Pill: How to Counteract the Conspiracy Theories That Are Killing Us by David Neiwert, 2020.

Republic of Lies: American Conspiracy Theorists and Their Surprising Rise to Power by Anna Merlan, 2019.

Squirrel Hill: The Tree of Life Synagogue Shooting and the Soul of a Neighborhood by Mark Oppenheimer, 2021.

The Big Lie: Election Chaos, Political Opportunism, and the State of American Politics after 2020 by Jonathan Lemire, 2022.

The Far Right Today by Cas Mudde, 2019.

The Flag and the Cross: White Christian Nationalism and the Threat to American Democracy by Philip S. Gorski and Samuel L. Perry, 2022.

The Storm Is Here: An American Crucible by Luke Mogelson, 2022.

The Storm Is Upon Us: How QAnon Became a Movement, Cult, and Conspiracy Theory of Everything by Mike Rothschild, 2021.

The Undertow: Scenes from a Slow Civil War by Jeff Sharlet, 2023.

They Knew: How a Culture of Conspiracy Keeps America Complacent by Sarah Kendzior, 2022.

They Want to Kill Americans: The Militias, Terrorists, and Deranged Ideology of the Trump Insurgency by Malcolm Nance, 2022.

This Will Not Pass: Trump, Biden, and the Battle for America's Future by Jonathan Martin and Alexander Burns, 2022.

Trust the Plan: The Rise of QAnon and the Conspiracy That Unhinged America by Will Sommer, 2023.

We Are Proud Boys: How a Right-Wing Street Gang Ushered in a New Era of American Extremism by Andy Campbell, 2022.

Index

n refers to a note

4chan (website) 16, 34, 42, 91, 146
4H (Head, Heart, Hands and Health) 135
8chan (message board) 51
8kun (website) 34, 91, 146
9/11 (11th September 2001) 108, 122, 141
"107" (Juan O Savin) 124, 176n7
2000 Mules (film) 19—22, 25, 44, 46, 72, 112, 155n12

abortion rights movement 37, 98
accelerationism 15, 90, 93—5, 154n9
Active Clubs 85
Adams, Dakota 2—4, 16—17, 146, 149
adrenochrome 58, 163n12
al-Fayoume, Wadea 118—9
al-Qaeda 94
alt-right 6—10, 30—1, 64, 85, 116
    opposition to 146—9
    see also far right
America First Secretaries of State Coalition 125, 140
Andreessen, Marc 154n9
Angeli, Jake 48—50, 56—7, 162n3
Anglin, Andrew 147—8
Anheuser-Busch company 62
Anti-Defamation League (ADL) 37, 88
anti-gay movement 63, 67
anti-progressivism 110—4, 116—20
anti-Semitism 30, 88, 115
anti-vaccine conspiracy theories 13—14, 70—5, 78—82, 110
antifa (anti-fascist movement) 64
Atomwaffen Division (neo-Nazi organization) 93
Anton, Michael 113

Ballard, Tim 57—8
ballot drop boxes 20—2
Baltimore attack on power stations (2023) 93
Bank Your Vote initiative 142
Bannon, Steve 54, 104, 111, 114, 144
Bardwell, Kedron 123, 133
Base, The (organization) 89
Beck, Glenn 114, 116—8
    The Great Reset 117—8
Bellingcat (organization) 34, 38, 42
Bezos, Jeff 45
Biden, Joe 6, 19, 52, 58, 141—2, 145—6
"Big Lie" 11, 120, 134
Biggs, Andy 36
Bikers for Trump (organization) 54
birthright citizenship 135—6
BitChute (website) 113
Black Lives Matter 59, 69, 100, 117
Black nationalism 36—7
Blaze, The (news website) 114, 116—7
Boogaloo Bois (anti-government movement) 93
Brand, Russell 111
Breitbart (news website) 101, 114
Bridgen, Andrew 79—80
Britain 5, 77—8, 79—80
Brody, Ben 84
Brookings Institution 37
Buffalo, NY mass shooting (2022) 35—6, 43

Capitol riot (6th January 2021) 4, 9—10, 48, 56, 59—60, 66, 85, 113, 140—1, 144—5
Carlson, Tucker 33, 37—8, 68—9, 111, 139—40, 156n5
Caviezel, Jim 58
Censorship Industrial Complex 109

Center for Strategic and International Studies 37
Cernovich, Mike 113
Charlottesville protest rally (2017) 10, 29–30, 148
Chauvin, Derek 156*n*5
Christian nationalism 95–105
Clendaniel, Sarah 93, 94
Clifford, Bennett 94
climate change conspiracy theories 45–6, 139
Clinton, Hillary 6, 8, 24, 50, 52, 145
Coeur d'Alene, Idaho Pride March (2022) 87
Comet Ping Pong restaurant 50
Community Notes (fact-checking service) 84
Connecticut 41, 67–8
conspiracy theories 23–5, 44, 138–9
conspiracy websites 106–7
Council on Foreign Relations 37
Covid-19 pandemic 5, 9, 70, 142–3
    and conspiracy theories 12–13, 45, 72–7, 139
    impact on children of 61–2
    see also anti-vaccine conspiracy theories
Crokin, Liz 54
Crowder, Steven 44

D'Souza, Dinesh 19, 20–1, 25–6, 154–5*n*5, 155–6*n*13
Daily Stormer (website) 147, 148
Daily Wire (news website) 114
deep state conspiracy theories 31–2, 44–5, 110, 144
Democratic Socialists of America 100
Department of Homeland Security 37, 40, 44
DeSantis, Ron 103, 104, 111, 141
Died Suddenly (film) 72, 73, 112
Dixon, Edie 63–4, 127
DLive (website) 113
Dominion (voting machine company) 114
Donny (Trump supporter) 130–2

Dore, Jimmy 111
drag story hours 61–2, 65, 66–7

@EducatingLiberals (Twitter account) 53
election
    (2016) 8, 24, 30
    (2020) 10, 11, 19–22, 46, 100, 122–5
    (2024) 15, 141–4
electoral system, distrust in 20, 22–3, 26, 132–4
Ellison, Larry 46
Engelbrecht, Catherine 21
Epps, Ray 66, 114
Epstein, Jeffrey 139

false equivalence 8, 31, 43
false flags 38–40, 83
Family Institute of Connecticut 67
far right 5–6, 10–11, 89, 145–6, 149
    opposition to 146–9
    see also alt-right
Federal Bureau of Investigation (FBI) 37, 40, 44, 66, 90, 126
Federal Reserve 53
Finchem, Mark 176*n*10
Fisher, Mark 154*n*9
Fletcher, Kimberly 101
Florida 88, 103, 111, 141
Floyd, George 33, 63, 93, 156–7*n*5,*n*6
Flynn, Michael 99–101, 104–5, 111, 144
Fox News 10, 37, 69, 101, 114
Fuentes, Nick 114, 163*n*7

Gab.com (website) 98, 113
Gates, Bill 45
Gateway Pundit (news website) 114
Gersh, Tanya 146–9
Gettr (social media platform) 113
Government Accountability Office 37
Goyim Defense League (GDL) 88
grand unified theory 47–58
Great Awakenings 97–8
great replacement theory 88

Great Reset, The (economic initiative) 90, 117–8, 136
Greene, Marjorie Taylor 80, 89, 119, 126
Greenwald, Glenn 111
Groypers (white nationalist movement) 114–5
gun ownership 3–4, 41

Halbig, Wolfgang 39–40
Hamas 119
Hamlin, Damar 71–2
Hard Reset, The (terrorist instruction manual) 90–1, 92
hate speech 118–9
Hawaii 45–6
Heyer, Heather 29–30, 32
Hindu nationalism 5
Hitler, Adolf 101, 103, 115
Hollow 2A, The 96–101, 104
House Freedom Caucus 11, 36, 111, 126–7

Idaho Pride March (2022) 87
incels 92–3
Indianola, Iowa 121
influencers 106–20
Infowars (online media outlet) 39–40, 115, 120
Institute for Strategic Dialogue 62
Iowa Caucus (2024) 99, 141
Iowa Republican Party 135–6
Israel/Palestine 119

Jackson County, Iowa 135
Jacksonville, Florida mass shooting (2023) 42–4, 137
Jefferson, Thomas 101
Jenner, Edward 14
Johnson, Dominique 68
Johnson, Mike 19–20
Jones, Alex 6, 39–40, 98, 107–9, 115, 116, 117–8, 129, 148
Jones, Kelly 107–9, 120
Jordan, Jim 126
Justice, Tiffany 103

Kennedy, Robert F. Jr. 111–2, 142
Khan, Veryan 94
Kirk, Charlie 119

Lahren, Tomi 116
Lake, Kari 125, 176*n*10
left-wing extremism 36–7
LGBTQ+ people 62, 67, 85
lone wolf killers 9, 92, 146
Loomer, Laura 113
Louisiana mass shootings (2016) 36–7

Marchant, Jim 124, 125, 140
mass murderer, sanctification of 92–3
mass terror attacks 30–1
    claims of fabrication of 39
    see also specific mass shootings, e.g. Sandy Hook
Matrix, The (film) 23
Maui, Hawaii wildfire (2020) 45–6
McCarthy, Kevin 126
McInnes, Gavin 65–7, 84, 86
Mellor, Vic 96–7, 100
Mencius Moldbug (blogger) *see* Yarvin, Curtis
Miller, Jason 113
Miller, Mary 101
Moms for America (organization) 101
Moms for Liberty (organization) 54, 101–4
Moonage Daydream (film) 19
motive denial 31, 33–5, 41
murder denial 31–3
Musk, Elon 34, 35, 38, 42, 84, 112, 148

Nashville, Tennessee mass shooting (2023) 43–4
Nationalist Front (organization) 89
Nazism 34, 115
neo-Nazis 34, 37, 41
New American (organization) 37
New Right 153*n*4
New York Times 34
New Yorker 117
Newsmax (news website) 101, 114
No Labels (organization) 142

non-falsifiable theories 50−1
North Carolina, attack on power stations (2022) 94
North Korea 140
Nunes, Devin 105

Oath Keepers 2, 14, 16, 26, 60, 86, 144
Obama, Barack 24, 27, 41, 45, 52, 99, 116, 117
Odnoklassniki (ok.ru) 34
Odysee (website) 113
Office, The (TV program) 52
One America News 101, 114
Operation Mocking Bird 50
Operation Underground Railroad 57
Operation Warp Speed 14, 80
Oregon City Pride march 83−6

Palestinians, attacks on 118−20
parental rights 62, 104
Parler (social network) 59, 113
Passion of the Christ, The (film) 58
Patriot Front (organization) 15, 84, 87−8, 89−90, 95
Patriot Prayer (Christian nationalist group) 128
pedophile conspiracy theories 51, 58, 61, 67−9, 109
Peters, Stew 72−4, 81
Peterson, Jordan 113
Pittsburgh Synagogue mass shooting (2018) 113
Pizzagate conspiracy theory 50−1, 54, 109
Plainfield, Ill. attack on Palestinians (2023) 118−9
Plandemic (film) 77
Podesta, John 50
Pool, Tim 111
Portland, Oregon 63−4, 127−9
Posobiec, Jack 103−4
Pressler, Scott 54
Pride events 62, 65, 67, 83, 87
Program on Extremism, George Washington University 37, 94
progressivism 110−1

Proud Boys (organization) 14, 16, 59−70, 104, 127−30, 144
Oregon City March (2023) 83−6
psychological operations (psyop) theories 31−2, 38−42, 49−50, 83

QAnon 12, 16, 48−58, 61, 98, 122, 124, 139, 176*n*7

Ramaswamy, Vivek 141
ReAwaken America movement 99−100, 104
Red Elephants (organization) 29, 156*n*1
Reddit 89
Revolver News (website) 114
Rhodes, Stewart 2−5, 17−18, 26, 60, 85, 86, 108, 145, 146, 155−6*n*13
Rittenhouse, Kyle 69
Roe v Wade 98
Rogan, Joe 111, 115−6
Rose City Nationalists 83
Roy, Chip 126
Rumble (video platform) 104, 112−3
Russell, Brandon 93, 94
Russia 34, 137

San Luis, Arizona 22
Sanders, Bernie 6, 115
Sandy Hook school shooting (2012) 39−41, 138
Sarasota County 104
Sardarizadeh, Shayan 34
school libraries, censorship of books in 62, 102
Secretary of State 125
Scranton, Pennsylvania 52−6
Shapiro, Ben 114
Shellenberger, Michael 112
Sisco, Michael 56, 163*n*7
Snell, Mark 123
Soros, George 32
Sound of Freedom (film) 57, 58
Spencer, Richard 8, 147−8
Spencer, Sherry 147
state secretaries of state, role of 125
stochastic terrorism 118−20

Stone, Roger 111
Sweasy, Amy 156n5

Taibbi, Matt 111, 112
Target (retail corporation) 62
Tarrio, Enrique 59–60, 65, 85
Telegram (app) 84, 85, 94, 146
Terrorgram movement 91–5
Terrorism Research and Analysis
    Consortium 94
terrorist groups, instruction manuals
    for 91–2
Texas black nationalist attack (2016)
    36–7
Texas mass shootings (2023) 33–5, 38
Thiel, Peter 46
Three Percenters Militia 14, 86
Toese, Tiny 128–9
Toler, Aric 34
transgender people 43, 61–4, 67
Trego, Montana 1–2, 17
True The Vote (organization) 20, 46
Trump, Donald
    for topics related to Donald Trump
    see the topic, e.g. Capitol riots;
    Proud Boys
Trump, Eric 105
Truth Social (social media platform)
    12, 98, 99, 104–5, 113
Twitch (gaming site) 35
Twitter see X

Ukraine: Russian invasion of 74, 110,
    140
Unite the Right (organization) 8
United States
    Constitution 96, 97
    separation of church and state
    97–8, 136
University of California, Berkeley
    protests 28–9
Uscinski, Joseph 24

Vancouver, Washington State 63
Vanguard America (neo-Nazi group)
    87
Vero Beach, Florida 72

Wakefield, Andrew 75, 79
Wall Street Journal 69
Warren County, allegations of voter
    fraud in 121–2, 133
Watch the Water (film) 73
Watkins, Jim and Ron 51
We Love Trump Keep America Great
    (tour) 53
Weiss, Bari 112
West, Cornel 142
West, Kanye 115, 148
Wheeler, Dylan 53, 55, 56–7
Whipple, David 122–4, 132–3
White House, driver attack on (2023)
    41–2
White Lives Matter 83, 87–8
white nationalism 87–8
white supremacy 15, 34, 37, 38, 94
Whitefish, Montana 147–8
wildfires conspiracy theories 45–6, 80
Winfrey, Oprah 45
Wisconsin 142–3
Witzke, Lauren 55–6, 72–3, 163n7
Wolf, Naomi 113
Wolfgang, Peter 67–8
Women for Trump (organization)
    54, 57
World Economic Forum 117
Wray, Chistopher 126–7

X 40, 42, 68–9, 89, 112

Yarvin, Curtis 113
YouTube 34

Ziegler, Bridget and Christian 104,
    172n17